A LONG WALK
with MARY

A Personal Search for the Mother of God

BRANDI WILLIS SCHREIBER

ANCIENT FAITH PUBLISHING ✤ CHESTERTON, INDIANA

A Long Walk with Mary: A Personal Search for the Mother of God
Copyright ©2021 Brandi Willis Schreiber

All rights reserved. No part of this publication may be reproduced by any means, electronic, mechanical, photocopying, recording, scanning, or otherwise, without the prior written permission of the Publisher.

Published by:
Ancient Faith Publishing
A Division of Ancient Faith Ministries
P.O. Box 748
Chesterton, IN 46304

All Old Testament quotations, unless otherwise identified, are from the Orthodox Study Bible, © 2008 by St. Athanasius Academy of Orthodox Theology (published by Thomas Nelson, Inc., Nashville, Tennessee) and are used by permission. New Testament quotations are from the New King James Version of the Bible, © 1982 by Thomas Nelson, Inc., and are used by permission.

ISBN: 978-1-944967-98-7

Library of Congress Control Number: 2021932893

Printed in the United States of America

First and foremost, for the Theotokos
I pray I have honored you with this book
And for David and Baby Rex Aidan, my beloveds,
And for all who are searching for the Mother of God
in their lives

Contents

Prayer to the Virgin Mary from the Akathist Hymn	7
Acknowledgments	9
Introduction	11
ONE ❋ Tears	18
TWO ❋ Strangers	28
THREE ❋ Prayers	42
FOUR ❋ Vessels	54
FIVE ❋ Mothers	65
SIX ❋ Holding Lightly	76
SEVEN ❋ Dryness	86
EIGHT ❋ Friends	96
NINE ❋ Miracles	104
TEN ❋ Wives	116
ELEVEN ❋ Sorrows	128
TWELVE ❋ Creation	139
THIRTEEN ❋ Guides of Grace	149
FOURTEEN ❋ Mourners	161
FIFTEEN ❋ The Return of the Prodigal	171
Epilogue	182
Additional Reading	188
Exploratory Questions	192
Endnotes	201

Prayer to the Virgin Mary
from the Akathist Hymn[1]

O SPOTLESS, UNDEFILED, INCORRUPTIBLE, chaste and pure Virgin-Bride of God, who by your wondrous conception united God the Logos with humankind, and joined our fallen nature with the Heavens; the only hope of the hopeless, and the help of the persecuted; the ever-ready to rescue all who flee unto you, and the refuge of all Christians: spurn me not, the accursed sinner, who by shameful thoughts, words, and deeds have made my whole being useless, and through indolence have enslaved my judgment to the pleasures of this life.

But, as the mother of the Merciful God, mercifully show compassion unto me, the sinner and prodigal, and accept my supplication offered unto you from impure lips.

With your maternal approach entreat your Son, our Lord and Master, to open for me the merciful depths of His lovingkindness; and overlooking my countless transgressions, guide me to repentance; and show me forth as a worthy worker of His commandments.

And be at my side always, as you are merciful, compassionate, and gentle; and in this present life be my fervent protectress and helper, thwarting the assaults of the adversaries, and leading me toward salvation; and at the hour of my passing take care of my wretched soul, and cast far away the dark faces of the evil demons.

And at the awesome Day of Judgment deliver me from eternal punishment and prove me an heir to the ineffable glory of Your Son and our God.

May this glory be my lot, O my lady, Most Holy Theotokos, through your mediation and help, by the grace and mercy of your Only-Begotten Son, our Lord and God, and Savior Jesus Christ; to whom is due all glory, honor, and worship, together with His Eternal Father and His All-Holy and Good and Life-giving Spirit, now and ever, and to the ages of ages. Amen.

Acknowledgments

IN THE YEAR I SPENT writing this book, many people gave me their unwavering support, surprised me with their love, or blessed me unknowingly. To you, I am eternally grateful.

I would first like to thank my husband, David, who believed in me, my writing, and this project from the very beginning. David, thank you for winnowing passages from your own studies to help me understand Mary better; for reading over drafts of this book and giving me your clear and concise feedback; for research trips to the university library (and Amazon!); and for helping me to see all the places in our lives where Mary lives and has worked for us. Most of all, thank you for loving me as I am. I love you more than you can ever know.

I would also like to thank my parish priest, the Reverend Father Peter DeFonce of St. Andrew Greek Orthodox Church in Lubbock, Texas, for blessing my writing and this work. Thank you, Father Peter, for your insight, support, conversations, and most of all, faith. You have kept me afloat in the darkest waters during the heaviest storms. And to all the wonderful people I know at St. Andrew: thank you for being excited for me and always asking about this project. It's my prayer that somehow this work will come back and bless you and our beloved parish tenfold.

To my amazing writing group, the Lone Star Women of Letters: There is no way I could have finished this book without your constant encouragement, positivity, feedback, and prayers. I love each of you to the moon and back. Thank you for being my women!

And lastly, special thanks go out to these individuals who encouraged and blessed me in unexpected ways and therefore had a part to play in this book's reality: Kristie Collins, Sonya Jensen, Kyla Shannon, Dr. Mary Carroll, and Melinda Johnson. Writing a book like this is soul-baring work. Thank you for seeing my soul and loving it anyway.

Introduction

*Ask, and it will be given to you; seek, and you will find;
knock, and it will be opened to you.*
—MATTHEW 7:7

As I write this, a cool breeze slips through the open window in my study, rustling a year's worth of notes and books about the Virgin Mary piled around my desk. A cold front has moved in after three days of summer rains, blessedly tempering what is normally our harshest season. The sky is gray and overcast; the branches of the pecan tree by our old shed dip and sway, making music in the wind. This beautiful morning, in which I can hear blue jays and sparrows call out to their kind over the treetops, is just one more good gift in a long season of receiving.

Ask, Christ preached in His Sermon on the Mount, and you will be given what you request. Seek what you know you are missing, and you will find it. Knock, and the door at which you stand will be opened to you. For over a year now, I have been asking, seeking, and knocking at the threshold of God's door to better understand the Virgin Mary and her purpose in my life and faith. My goal was simple, or so I thought: ask to know her better, seek knowledge and experience of her, knock so that I might meet her. By learning about her role in my Eastern Orthodox faith, I hoped to acquire a better understanding, appreciation, and respect for her I didn't have before I became Orthodox in 2009—and, quite honestly, for a long period after I became Orthodox.

But "how much more" has my Father given to me in this process (Matt. 7:11 OSB).

When I first told my friends and family I was writing a book about my search for Mary, their responses ranged from genuine interest and support to uncertainty. More often than not, I got a polite "Oh, that's interesting," but a few people boldly asked, "Why?" I honestly liked this latter response better because, really, what *is* the point of writing a book about an Orthodox convert's year searching for Mary? Who would want—or need—a book like this? The underlying context of most people's responses, however, subtly highlighted a prevalent attitude that surrounds Mary in many circles of believers and nonbelievers alike: Why, really, does she matter?

In my evangelical Protestant background, Mary was regarded as just a minor player in the Bible, if she was regarded at all. She had a purpose and a place—to give birth to Christ and to appear on pretty Christmas cards—but that was about it. No mention was made of her life or her importance, other than being the best option, perhaps, for a womb and young mother. Worse, I sensed a hostility about her. I remember gazing upon a picture of her painted in calming tones in a hallway of my Catholic best friend's home. I sensed a peace about her; she appeared at home in that dark nook and not at all dangerous. But talking about her provoked defensive reactions from others. I received the message clearly: Why would anyone need to know about Mary at all?

In his lovely book *Mary, Worthy of All Praise: Reflections on the Virgin Mary*, Fr. David Smith makes the bold statement that "every culture must confront her mystery . . . every Christian must face the debt we have to her."[2] I thoroughly believe this is true, regardless of what faith background we come from. Whatever personal thoughts and feelings people have about her, she *does* have a part in the story of Christ's life, in Christianity as a whole, and in our salvation. But how do I confront her mystery? Where do I even begin to acknowledge that debt?

These are the monumental questions that started the journey whose chronicle you are holding in your hands or listening to now. In all my research and reading on Mary, I found many great academic and theological resources devoted to her (some of which I have listed for your reference in the Additional Reading section), but not a lot of stories, essays, or books about regular people who "met" her in their modern lives or wanted to incorporate devotion to her but weren't sure how to start. I especially couldn't find any books written for converts on this topic; zero exist from an Orthodox perspective. As someone who is a writer and consumer of stories, I was hungry to learn from others how they've met Mary in their lives, but I couldn't find much that spoke directly to me: a woman living in the modern world who is an ordinary Orthodox Christian, and a convert to boot.

So I decided to "confront her mystery . . . and face the debt" as best I could on my own. As I learned about Mary, I prayed and I wrote. What follows is my story of what happened over my year of searching and how she undoubtedly not only influenced my life, but also helped strengthen my overall faith, my love of God, and my spiritual practice, particularly my prayer life.

However, I know this story isn't complete. As a convert to Eastern Orthodoxy, I am most definitely no expert on Mary, the Orthodox Church, its theology, or the two thousand years of history that shaped our tradition. I haven't been to seminary or earned an advanced degree in divinity; nor do I work in a church or ministerial setting in my day job. I am an ordinary person, trying to live out my faith as best I can with the resources I have access to—including life in my small West Texas parish, guidance from my priest, and the wealth of knowledge available to me through the history and tradition of the Church. That means there are no doubt things in this book I have gotten wrong or misinterpreted, and so I sincerely ask the reader to be gracious with me if I have erred.

As Evagrius of Pontus said, the "one who prays truly will be a theologian, and the one who is a theologian will pray truly."[3] This has been the guiding principle for everything I've written over the last year, and I hope it helps you, as well, as you seek your own answers, understanding, and relationship with Mary.

MEMOIR IS ONE OF MY favorite genres. There is something life-altering and profound about following someone's personal story and discovering what happens when she pulls her life experiences into the light, examines them, and hopefully, is changed by this process. If we are honest with ourselves, writing our story should be transformative for us as the author, but the experience should also be transformative for the reader, for the reader becomes emotionally involved and (hopefully) likewise transformed by the author's journey.

However, as Mary Karr writes in *The Art of Memoir*, "The form *always* has profound psychological consequence on its author . . . there's suffering involved."[4] A journey like this is not one that comes without pain, sacrifice, and consequences (for the author *and* the reader, I would add). A year in anyone's life is going to be filled with a whole lot of ups and downs, but that is compounded when you add a spiritual element to it. When you *really* invite God into your life and ask Him and His saints for help, Christ promises in Matthew 7:7 that you'll get an answer. And how He will answer! That invitation you extend, as I learned, is going to peel back your skin and make you see who you really are beneath and what you struggle with that continually separates you from God's love and from other people. In other words, it is going to hurt.

"God's love is remorseless," Metropolitan Anthony Bloom writes in *Courage to Pray*. He's warning his readers not to seek out mystical experiences, but rather, to seek "repentance and conversion"—a turning back to God, which should always be the focus of any encounter we wish to have with our Creator. Doing this means that we continually cry out, "Lord[,] make me what I should be, change me whatever the cost," and God will answer.[5]

Ultimately, an encounter with Mary *is* an encounter with our Creator. Praying to the Theotokos, seeking her help, and honoring who she is in the role of our salvation is not "idol worship," as some have said to me. In the Orthodox Christian perspective, a contemplation on Mary is *always*

Christological, that is, Christ-centered. We don't look to Mary as a divine entity or as someone who is worthy of worship because of her own power, like a goddess; and we most certainly don't put her above the Father, the Son, or the Holy Spirit. Rather, we look to her because she points the way, often quite literally as depicted in many of her icons, to Christ. The whole of her life and experience exists, thanks to her open and willing participation, to make our salvation possible. To this end, we owe her much gratitude and praise.

And that's really the crux of this book. As Fr. David Smith notes, "Every generation of Christians must make Mary . . . their own."[6] The pages that follow are my attempt to make her my own: to pay attention to her, learn about her, participate in the life of the Church with her, pray to her, ask her questions, seek her help, thank her, and most importantly, give her the respect and honor she is due.

This journey changed my life and continues to do so. It is my sincere hope that whoever reads these pages or listens to these words may be edified and learn something from my experience, too, should God be so gracious as to use me for this purpose. Maybe you'll gain a different way of thinking about the Mother of God or details of her life you might not have given a second thought before. Maybe you'll find a new prayer or resource you can incorporate into your own spiritual practice. Maybe you'll simply discover something about yourself in the process of reading about my questions, struggles, and hopes or from the Exploratory Questions in the back. My deepest prayer, however, is that this book helps at least one person meet Mary in a new way—whether you be Orthodox "cradle" or convert, a Christian from another tradition, or just a curious reader.

Introduction

As I finish typing this and look out across the green of my little yard and hear the mourning doves coo into the afternoon, I pray that your heart may be opened to the great blessings we receive when we "ask . . . seek . . . [and] knock." May the peace of Christ be with you.

❋ ONE ❋

Tears

Without tears our dried heart could never be softened, nor our soul acquire spiritual humility, and we would not have the force to become humble.
—SAINT SYMEON THE NEW THEOLOGIAN[7]

Somewhere west of the Brazos River and northeast of the Davis Mountains, the Texas landscape changes from green, rolling hills awash in prairie shortgrass and settles into the flat, high plains characteristic of this region. West Texas stretches in all directions, like a blanket pulled at invisible corners by the weight of endless blue sky. No natural monuments, no height of forest or mountain or stone rises above the horizon out here; all that is varied and interesting, some say, exists in the ancient canyon systems spread throughout this region, invisible until you halt at their sudden precipices and stare down into their chasms.

In the winter, this *llano estacado*, or "staked plains" as the early explorers named it, is stripped bare of its rare green and fades into the gold-and-gray of frost-killed blue grama and buffalo grass. Spring is a season of bloom and wind: dust storms, fueled by westerly currents, paint the sky red with iron-heavy dust and leave everything, including the tender, unfurling leaves of mesquite and maple, covered in a gritty film. In the summer, the days hum in dizzying eighty-, ninety-, and hundred-degree heat, and the slow, sleepy clatter of cicadas staccatos the air. Autumn might be the only tolerable season, yet it lasts only a few weeks. The falling leaves, cooling temperatures, and last rains of the year elapse between late October and mid-November, until everything turns gold and gray again.

It is in the midst of this lonely, windswept plain of Texas, where it seems most people are either passing through or passing on, that I have become Orthodox.

This is also the place in which I have asked Mary, the Mother of God, to become real to me for the first time, in ways she never has before.

Before.

I pause at the word. What is the *before*? Humans like to think of conversions as jostling events that recast life into *what was* and *what is now*, as if time were split in two. Perhaps that's true for some, but my conversion, my movement into an awareness of mystery greater than my Protestant background allowed, has not been the sudden flipping on of a light, a too-bright moment stunning me into waking from a darkness of sleep. Rather, it has been the slow shift into morning, illuminating by degrees what I could not see before from shades of ash into life-giving white. I say *has been*, for it is an ever-evolving experience, each day fresh with revelations and challenges, mercy and grace. Almost like a long drive into a solitary plain with only the scissortails, fleeing coyotes, and warm air rushing by my open window for company.

THE LIGHTS ARE DIM IN our beloved but well-worn parish church. It is the first week of Great Lent, ten years ago, and I am participating in the service of Small Compline, followed by the Akathist Hymn to the Theotokos, the Virgin Mary. The service is long, and I am twenty-eight years old. At this particular Pascha, I will finally be chrismated. I have been anticipating this for a long time.

For months now, I have watched the rest of the congregation line up at the end of the Divine Liturgy for the Eucharist. This is different, I learn, from the commemoration of my youth done "in remembrance" of the Lord's Last Supper. The Eucharist is revelatory, for it is the real Body and Blood of Christ manifest in real bread and wine. While the parishioners partake, I stand respectfully, watching carefully but trying not to stare, knowing I am so close to something I want but cannot yet fully receive.

I have come to all the services this week because it is my first Great Lent, and I don't want to miss anything. It is late in the evening, the sun disappearing behind the junipers that line our parish's cracked parking lot. Only candles and a few electric lamps over the iconostasis illuminate the church, and the failing light shifts into a smoky gray hue with the drifting of incense. A streetlamp outside backlights the stained-glass windows, and my attention shifts between the emerald and ruby glass, the pages of our service book, and the icons on the walls.

They are easy to study, these visual depictions of Orthodox theology. As a catechumen, I don't know much about these icons, and I hardly understand their meaning (this will take years), but I recognize they are holy. Hung in small arrangements around the room, they are there for me to examine and contemplate, and I appreciate that. I think about what's happening in each one; I remember they embody a cloud of saints surrounding us, real and present. I talk to some of them in my head.

The icon of Christ is easiest for me to relate to. Jesus, after all, was the sole focus of the evangelical background in which I grew up. But this service tonight is specifically for the Theotokos, the Mother of God. Her icon is positioned across from the icon of Christ, on my left on the iconostasis, directly in my line of view tonight. Because of this, I look at it more often.

The icon is beautiful, framed in the same gold paint as the icon of Christ. Her features are strong, her expression soft but unreadable, conveying neither smile nor frown. Yet it is not detached: the same as the icon of Christ. However, unlike Christ, whose body is positioned full-front to the viewer, the Theotokos's head is tenderly inclined toward the Christ Child she holds in her lap while she looks into the room. Her attention is double-focused on the One through whom all things were created, her Son, *and* the created ones, the people here in this tiny parish in a town that mostly doesn't even know it exists.

I am one of those people. Still a newlywed, but not yet a mother, I am trying to navigate new relationships, the changing landscape of my late twenties, and some kind of career. My father has not yet died, and weekends my parents still gather at my house for dinner, games, and late-evening laughter. I am not yet Orthodox but striving to be (it will take me years to understand what the striving means). I don't know the Greek words of the Divine Liturgy; I have only memorized their phonetic sounds so I can chant along. I hardly understand the saints or what it means to be in a community of them. This is my first Small Compline and Akathist Hymn service, and it is inexplicably beautiful, but I don't really know what's happening. I am reading, participating, and praying with those gathered on this shadowy evening, but I feel grossly inadequate because there is still *so much* to learn.

Through this, the Mother of God, in an icon as large and beautiful as her Son's, is waiting silently on the wall in front of me. Looking at me, it seems. But I don't really know who she is.

I don't know *how* to know who she is.

My priest, who patiently guides my husband and me on our Orthodox journey, asks me to read the Prayer to the Theotokos, one of the final prayers of this lengthy service, in front of her icon. He is giving me as a catechumen every opportunity to participate, but I still feel lost. And perhaps a little unworthy.

I swallow and step forward.

"O spotless, undefiled, incorruptible, chaste and pure Virgin Bride of God," I begin, "who by your wondrous conception united God the Logos with humankind and joined our fallen nature with the Heavens; the only hope of the hopeless, and the help of the persecuted . . . ever-ready to rescue all who flee unto you, and the refuge of all Christians . . ."[8]

I address Mary in a way I never have before. I speak and pray to "the only hope of the hopeless."

This hits me. So often I feel hopeless, not sure if my enough is enough, if I am doing the right thing and living my life as best I should. I have spent years praying to God in long, rambling prayers, most of which comprise some version of "If You could just please . . ." I have fled plenty of times to God, mostly in times of need. Needing His protection. Needing His power. Needing whatever He can do at that particular juncture of my life that I cannot. I am no stranger to those types of prayers. But yet I know deep down I am always getting it wrong.

But this is different. This prayer is . . . *not about me*. This is a structured prayer of recognition, ancient and established, that lauds the virtues and importance of Mary. She is important in ways I have never recognized. She's present and worthy of such a prayer.

I read the words "the refuge of all Christians," and something shifts in my chest. I feel it move, like a small, sleeping animal waking behind bars. I continue: "Spurn me not, the accursed sinner, who by shameful thoughts, words, and deeds have made my whole being useless . . . but, as the mother of the Merciful God, mercifully show compassion unto me, the sinner and prodigal."

The Prodigal Son is one of my favorite parables. The squanderer who leaves Love in his broken-hearted wake fails, suffers, and returns to the same Love that never stopped hoping or waiting for his return. I am a prodigal, too: desperate to leave a version of God that feels incomplete and instead find wholeness, fullness, and belonging in something else. This is why I am converting to Orthodox Christianity after years of searching and feeling like an outcast in my religious community. Leaving all I know is a painful process, especially because my family does not understand my decision. In time, most of them will be supportive. But on this particular night, I am both exhilarated and scared. I have never prayed this kind of prayer before, certainly not to Mary, who in my past religious experience was only discussed in sermons at Christmastime or was characterized as having a fleeting, small role in the bigger story of Christianity. I did not know I could pray a prayer like this to Mary.

I did not know she would listen.

"And be at my side always, as you are merciful, compassionate, and gentle," I read.

She can be near to me? The Mother of God, the person in the story of salvation that I perhaps understand the least, is near to *me*? This also is new. God is near to me, I know, and certainly Christ through His Father. However, I have not had this kind of female spiritual closeness before. I'm not even sure what that means, but I go on.

> *And in this present life be my fervent protectress and helper, thwarting the assaults of the adversaries, and leading me toward salvation; and at the hour of my passing take care of my wretched soul, and cast far away the dark faces of the evil demons. And at the awesome Day of Judgment deliver me from eternal punishment and prove me an heir to the ineffable glory of your Son and our God. May this glory be my lot, O my lady, Most-Holy Theotokos, through your mediation and help.*

I feel something pressing against my rib cage, and the newly wakened animal within breaks through at these words. Suddenly, I am wracked with tears as I read. I ask for her help, protection, intercession, and everything else listed in the prayer as I read on. I stumble through the litany of things I didn't know I could ask of the Mother of God with a cracking, strained voice.

I know without understanding that what I am praying is true. I know, deep down, that she is virtuous, and I know that I am in sorry need of help. I barely get through it, however, and can hardly lift my eyes to her icon when I finish reading. Mary looks back with that same soft expression, but this time I see tenderness. This time I *feel* the compassion, understand there is some kind of mercy working in this moment. It is as if she is saying to me, "I see you." I have never felt so seen before, so exposed. I can't hide here.

My sight blurs. I finish the prayer, stumble likewise through an awkward veneration (I am learning that, as well), and step away.

"It happens to me every time I read it, too," a beloved member of my parish tells me later. And it does. It ends this way the next time I am asked to read the Prayer to the Virgin Mary during this service, ten years later. I break into tears before her icon and weep again while the gray light shifts further into black. While the candles burn down, and the incense dissipates, and the traffic outside fades to a subtle hum, I read and cry while the other women of the church cry, too.

※

IT IS THIS PARTICULAR READING of the Prayer to the Virgin Mary, ten years later, that has prompted my deeper search for the Mother of God. This particular year is saturated with sorrow. I am at a time in my life when I am the most broken I have ever been, and while stuttering through the words, I am yet again overcome with a sense of being intimately observed, a looking-into of the status of my heart.

It is not a new feeling this time. This year I have become

soft and open, like an overripe peach that will burst if pressed too much. I cry easily, especially at church. An overriding sense of grief and grace fills my days, and it is my small parish, the love of family and friends, and my evolving faith that pull me through this difficult season, hour by hour. My faith, in fact, has deepened greatly over this difficult year, so I'm surprised how emotional I am as I read the Prayer to the Virgin Mary. But the sorrow is deeper this year, the tenderness more acute. I feel Mary is really listening and understands, and again, I feel unworthy.

My reading becomes so fractured that my priest comes to my side and comforts me. He knows it has been a difficult year. At this tiny parish I am safe to be vulnerable, and I understand that tears are a natural part of this exchange. I finish reading, venerate her icon, and back away, but I feel I have approached an invisible yet palpable edge. I can't see it, but I know I am on the precipice of something: a canyon, perhaps, or a great chasm I am about to traverse.

Why has Mary not felt so close before? What is this intimacy I have missed with her, except in these brief moments, despite being Orthodox for nearly ten years?

Mary, clearly, is here. She surrounds me. Icons of her hang in church, in my home, even in my car, and stand on my bedside table. We chant and pray to her every Sunday; we read and learn about her in homilies. She is part of the daily prayers, mentioned over and over again.

I know the problem isn't lack of access to Mary. It's me accessing *her*. I've glossed over these teachings and focused on other things, spiritual or not, that vie for my attention. I'm the one who hasn't shown up or taken the time to understand what relationship with her could be. I haven't pursued her or made her a real spiritual priority in my life, despite ten years of being Orthodox.

And the "why" of that bothers me more. The honest truth is, I don't know what it means to rely on her and trust in her faithfulness and intercessions, so I haven't tried. I haven't learned to turn to her, to pray to her in earnest, or to seek her out. I don't think I've yet trusted—or believed—that I could.

In fact, I wonder if I might even be a little afraid of her.

The truth of this washes over me as I wipe the last tears from my cheeks. I don't know Mary that well, but I *want* to know her. The Father was always waiting for the prodigal to return home.

Could it be that Mary has been waiting for me, too?

I feel an old nudge.

"I see you," she seems always to be saying. "Are you ready to see me?"

I know my *yes* will change everything.

❋ TWO ❋

Strangers

> *Prayer is a golden link connecting the Christian man, the wanderer and the stranger upon earth, with the spiritual world of which he is a member, and, above all, with God the Source of life.*
> —SAINT JOHN OF KRONSTADT[9]

I AM DRIVING TO A small village in New Mexico to spend four days. The long fall and spring semesters are over, and my work helping college students with disabilities at the university where I'm employed has entered the lightest workload period of the year: blessed summer. Almost all of my students have left for home, internships, or classes at their local community colleges, and although my office is still open, I have this week of sweet respite before the summer terms begin.

It is midmorning, the sky shrouded in varying textures of bruise-colored clouds, and I am heading west, my car pointed like an arrow toward two hundred fifty miles of needle-straight road that will lead me into the Sierra Blanca Mountains.

I am in heaven.

On long road trips, I am in suspended homelessness, absent from the comfortable thresholds I have left and the not-quite-arrived-at destinations. It is one of my favorite times to think, wonder, and lose myself in the fields sliding past. I sing loudly with every song on the radio (and learn new ones). Growing up in West Texas, where hours pass between towns, you learn how to drive at a young age and make the most of long stretches. I yearn for these distances and the feeling of being in the middle of nowhere when I have been in town too long, deep in the daily work of life. I long for trips in which the old world dissolves and I become a stranger in a strange land, at least for a little while.

My car passes over the state line into New Mexico, and I slow to accommodate the lower speed limit. The two-lane road I am driving, the only major thoroughfare into the small mountain village where I will stay, shifts through farmland in neat rows of irrigated corn and sorghum into the brushy, sandy plains where only wild yucca, cacti, and mesquite thrive. Pronghorn deer graze among herds of cattle, their black horns curving up gracefully into hearts above their heads. What beauties they are. I squeal when I pick them out of the herds and remember when once, years ago, coming back from Santa Fe on a country road, my husband and I happened upon a herd of them moving like a wave down the slope of an escarpment. They seem to like it out here, for this part of eastern New Mexico is rarely delineated with barbed-wire fences.

I like it, too. A female pronghorn lifts her head as I pass, and I notice a tiny fawn standing in the shadow of her belly. I glance at the small icon of Mary I have tucked into my cupholder and thank her for this mothering, although I still have no children of my own.

The Theotokos and I are the only other travelers on this road.

Soon I drive through Roswell, a quirky little town boasting alien artwork, wine tastings, and an historic main street, and continue on. Eventually the flat, skull-bleached terrain shifts into angular, rocky hills the color of wheat. I am at the foothills of the mountains. Toward the northwest, I can see the peak of South Arabela, a lonely, dark mountain jutting from the horizon, but I head southwest instead, toward the Mescalero Reservation and into the mountain pass of the Sierra Blanca range. Nearly two hours later on winding roads that take me higher, higher, higher, I stop in front of my tiny cabin, an internet rental find tucked among piñon pines and white firs on a lurching incline.

The air here is sweet and high, and it is wonderfully chilly for May; I pull on a sweater as I unload my car. This trip was a gift from my husband: four days of reading, hiking, and whatever else I can do to "be as close to God as possible." I have come for rest and reflection, as well as challenge, for I have never been on a trip like this before. I am alone, and that frightens me a little. I do not fear crime in this small mountain village, but rather, I'm afraid I won't do this time justice. I have been craving solitude and time in nature, and although this trip was my husband's idea, I feel a little selfish about being here while the rest of life goes on back home. It is an old problem I have: lacking balance between taking care of myself and taking care of everything else, and feeling guilty for failing at both things.

Plus, I'm a little unsure of what to expect on a solo trip

like this. What do I *do*? I look down at the floor, where I have set two bags full of books, journals, drugstore beauty treatments, and my hiking boots—all suggestions from my friends and family of what to bring for a personal retreat. It is a glorious gift, this gift of time, and I don't want to waste it by being frozen in inaction or overplanning (another quality with which I struggle). I feel off-kilter, humbled that I'm here, and use the quiet of the cabin to center myself. I take a deep breath and remind myself it's okay for once to just *be*.

I bring in the last of my belongings and set up a small icon corner next to my bed, placing my little handmade icon of Mary, something I found on a work trip, next to a candle. I keep this icon on my nightstand at home and bring it with me anytime I travel.

"Okay, we're here," I say, and then I feel dumb because of course we're here. She knows that already, but I am reminded of something my priest told me when I asked how to pray to my patron saint.

"Just talk to her," he told me. It was simple, common-sense advice, but it highlighted a fear I had that as a new Orthodox Christian I would "do it wrong," this getting to know the saints. I already felt awkward, suspecting I lacked some inherent knowledge that lifelong Orthodox had about natural interactions with the saints. Is it easier for people growing up Orthodox to engage with them? Or does everyone, regardless of their background, struggle with this?

Mary, her face painted the same way it has been for nearly sixteen hundred years, tenderly returns my gaze. For some reason, this gives me comfort. I know what to expect when I look at her. When I stumble and fall in my life, my own inconsistencies abounding, I know I can trust what is never-changing. I can learn what she's trying to teach me. The lessons are available to me, if I'm just willing to be open to them.

In fact, in Orthodox Christianity, a whole history of the Church, including millennia of believers, saints, and tradition, is open to me. A staggering swath of church history, knowledge, and teaching was absent in my previous faith, and this is one of the things that drew me to Orthodoxy in the first place. I craved the context, to understand why we did certain things, believed certain things. Becoming Orthodox means that for the first time in my life I feel a direct, uninterrupted connection with the early believers and those who established the Faith. Before (there is that word again), my faith felt like an already-arrived-at destination, in which the journey and the landscape didn't matter. That journey avoided a great mountain range of questions, hidden in darkness and clouds, that I was always told to bypass.

But in finding Orthodox Christianity, the vital pass that had been closed for years was finally open, and I could traverse it for the first time, overcome with all there was to see, learn, and experience, including the peaks and valleys of faith.

It's this consistency, this tradition, that removes the ego-laden concern that I'm "doing it wrong" and allows me instead to rely on the teaching of the Church. Part of this involves communication with the saints and with everyone else who has gone before.

So I talk to Mary here in my tiny cabin in a mountain village far from home, and I thank her for a safe trip and ask her to show herself to me over the next four days. It's not a test, but rather a request for what I know I may fail to see on my own. "We often receive through prayer that which we have asked for, especially when we pray for that which relates to the salvation of our soul," St. John of Kronstadt wrote.[10]

It is a request I will make many times in the next year: something, I soon learn, that will be answered in abundance.

※

ON DAY TWO, I STRETCH my legs after a long writing session and decide to leave the quiet coffee shop I've found on the edge of a river and explore the village main street. Quaint storefronts beckon with handmade soaps, candles, and local artistry, and I've avoided them so far because these stores sell exactly the kind of thing that speaks to my weakness. I am trying to be as economical as possible on this trip, so I decide I'll just walk and browse for writing inspiration for an hour before heading back to my spot on the coffee shop's deck. I tuck my writing bag into my car and walk down the road, my purse tightly zipped.

Almost immediately, I am drawn to a stucco building with bright green trim. Religious paraphernalia, crosses, and sparkling silver jewelry hang in its windows. I am here right before the tourist season officially begins, but the abbreviated hours on the store's sign indicate it's open.

I step inside, just to look, of course.

The shop is small, and I think I am the only one here until I hear a sound above my head. A middle-aged woman dressed in a long olive-colored dress, crisply pressed and cinched with a bright belt at her waist, glides down the stairs. I recognize immediately that she must be the owner and the artist, for her hands, wrists, and neck sparkle with the same chunky silver pieces displayed in the store's cabinets. Her red hair, almost the same shade as her lips, is slicked into an elegant bun.

"Hello!" she says with a rich accent I can't immediately place. "Welcome!" I am struck by her grace and beauty, of course, but also by her warmth, which is decidedly motherly. Her big eyes search me, and she seems genuinely glad I have entered her shop—and not, I intuit, because she's hoping for a sale.

"Hello," I return. "This is a beautiful store. Are these your pieces?" I ask, although I already know the answer to my question.

"Yes, yes," she says. "I make all this jewelry, except for the crosses." She motions to the floor-to-ceiling crucifixes and wooden crosses in a variety of colors, shapes, and sizes hanging from the walls and pillars. "These come from all over New Mexico and Mexico."

I begin to wander, and I notice Mary is here, too. Tiny statues of the Madonna robed in blue peek from between display shelves of jewelry and scarves. Some of the statues look well-loved and worn, as if they were plucked right from an old Catholic church, while others are more modern in style. All of them remind me of the Madonnas I saw in the home of my best friend growing up; they fill me with a sense of love. This shop owner does, too. She takes me around her store and shows me the pieces she's made.

Her workmanship is beautiful. Bangles and rings and necklaces are heavy with detail, gemstones, and . . . price. I have no doubt they are worth every penny, but I have pushed my wallet to the bottom of my purse for a reason. The owner, who tells me her name, doesn't seem fazed at all when I drift toward a little rack of bracelets *much* lower in price. They lack the intricate artistry in the store's other pieces and seem to have a different story. The owner's voice follows me when I pause to look.

"My mother made those. She lived to be ninety-four and worked right alongside me in this store for years," she tells me. "She had a long and beautiful life. *Bea-u-ti-ful!*" She emphasizes the word. "A beautiful life!"

"Really?" I finger a bracelet. It's strung with colorful plastic beads, the kind you might find at a craft store, and I'm touched by the thought of this woman's mother working right alongside her, making her own jewelry and selling it in this remote mountain village with her daughter.

"Oh, yes. She'd follow me around here and arrange all the jewelry, wipe down all the counters." Her accent draws out *je-wel-ry* and *coun-ters*, and I envision her mother doing those things. Perhaps she was vibrant and quick in her work; perhaps she was slow and methodical. I can see it either way.

"I lost her exactly a year ago," the owner says, interrupting my thoughts, "and I miss her terribly."

I stop and look at her. "Oh, I'm so sorry," I say. I genuinely am. I know what it is like to lose a parent. This year my own father will have been gone for nine years. The loss and the grief's lasting effects on my mom have been difficult.

"Oh, yes," she says again, slicing a hand through the air. "I haven't even been able to clean out her studio. I left everything"—she motions in front of her, as if to emphasize a worktable covered with piles of her mother's beads and unfinished projects—"exactly as she left it. I just can't bear to put it up." Her eyes shine with unshed tears. "But you know," she continues, "God has a plan for everything. His timing is *perfect*."

I still, and I feel a tingling at the back of my neck. I believe in that divine timing, too, and I believe in the magic of interactions with strangers. "Entertaining angels" and all that. My father was kind to everyone he met. No one was too poor or too lowly for his respect, and he taught me that lesson. Once, not long before he died, I stopped in a convenience store with him to buy a soda, and I was surprised by how well he knew the checkout clerk. It turns out he talked to her every time he came in. He genuinely cared about her life and her family. "Your dad is a nice man," she told me in a gravelly voice as we turned to leave. "He always asks how I'm doing." How much that had meant to her, and how much the memory means to me now.

I believe that every person is sent to us for a reason, and in this tiny shop full of Marys, I start to feel the purpose of this interaction unfolding.

"I believe that, too," I tell the owner, and the connection opens us to deep, meaningful conversation. She begins to tell me about all the instances in her life when she believed that things could not have happened any other way, because of God's timing and providence.

"My mother," she tells me, "was never sick. No cancer, no heart problems, nothing! But she died while I was away visiting my daughter. I think deep down she knew that I could not have handled it if she'd died here with me, so she went back to her home in Mexico while I went away to visit my daughter overseas. And when I stepped off the plane, I had a phone call from my brother. She'd died while I was in the air!" She practically yells this. "In the air! She died while I was over the *o-ce-an*, in a place where God knew there was nothing that I could do. And I stop, and I cry. I think to myself, 'What do I do now? I'm all the way over here.' But I have my daughter and my three grandbabies to visit, so I stay. Nothing I could do," she reemphasizes. "But God knew what He was doing. That was the only way it could have happened."

She is speaking about mercy, being spared what we cannot handle, and I understand this, too. So many times I have looked back on events in my life to try to understand why they happened the way they did, as if understanding every miniscule cause and effect would help me to make better sense of everything, and therefore, to better cope. Loss, death, suffering, and pain. Opportunities, life, love, and hope: everything could only have occurred exactly the way it did. The decisions that led me to the university I attended, where I ended up meeting my husband. The random connections that helped us both get jobs and start careers. The places I was when I learned of good news, deaths, possibilities. The moments when my heart was pierced through by those supposed to love me the most and I thought I couldn't go on. The unfailing, unexpected grace that pulled me through each and every one of those moments.

None of it could have happened without God, not any other way. No matter how much my rational brain tries to make sense of the "why" and the "how," I know that I'll never possess the ability to see things from God's perspective. I'm not supposed to, for I am not God, but that doesn't mean Love is absent. As if I need more proof of this, I remember I am standing in this warm, beautiful store, where the owner and I are illuminated, I imagine, with the unobservable light of two believers gathered together. I think again of crying in front of the icon of Mary, and of my difficult year, and how those things, too, have brought me to this moment.

None of this could have happened any other way.

"Take my daughter, for instance," the owner continues. "She met her husband in a *jungle*." She laughs. "A jungle! They were both there traveling. She was walking up a road with a friend, and this boy comes walking down the same road with a friend. They meet on the road. She ends up marrying him. That was fifteen years ago! You couldn't dream that up!"

I smile because, yes, I understand. Some of the best things that have happened to me were things I would never have been able to choreograph, not in my wildest dreams.

"Any idea we have that *we* are in control—that is an illusion." She waves her hand again in the air, as if to dismiss such a silly notion.

"And what about you?" she asks abruptly. She wants to know about my life, why I am here, and where I'm from. But it's hard for me to answer her because I'm still thinking about not being in control. For some reason, that observation cuts close to the quick. I think about a quote from one of the Church Fathers (I can't remember his name) that goes something like "we need to relax into God's hands." I have been trying hard to do that, acutely aware during this part of my life that I can't control other people or the circumstances around me. All I can control is what I do, how I treat others, and how I respond to what happens to me. By "letting go and letting God," as another saying goes, I am relinquishing the illusion that I have any power over what happens to me or that my life is outside the power and providence of God—a sneaky lie of the evil one frequently whispered into my ear. It is both a terrifying and a solacing acceptance, this total trusting in God.

The fact that I am not very good at it hints, too, at my lack of faith in the power of other things, like prayers, saints, and intercessions. I am just now learning what it *really* means to trust God. Perhaps part of that lesson is learning what it means to trust Mary, as well.

I glance at another Madonna poised on a shelf behind the owner and again feel an incredible mercy around me. I am learning. I am trying and failing most days, but I am still here, and so is Mary. My prayer to see her on this trip is already answered. How could it be otherwise?

And then to my horror and embarrassment, I start to cry.

"Oh, no. No, no, no," the owner begs. "Please don't cry." Her eyes widen with alarm, and I feel stupid and weak for crying in front a stranger, although at this point, she feels less like a stranger and more like a friend. However, I can't stop. Tenderness, tenderness is all around me, and I let it rush over and through me. The owner produces a box of tissues from somewhere and comforts me, and then the little brass bell over her door rings, and another customer steps in.

She stops short once inside. "I'm sorry. Am I interrupting something?" the customer asks, casting confused glances between me and the owner. I can't help but quietly chuckle. If only she knew. I shake my head and use the opportunity to move away from the counter while the owner retrieves the customer's order. I look more closely at the crosses on the walls.

Of course, at this point, I have to buy one. It is the least I can do to thank this woman, this stranger, who has spent the better half of an hour talking faith, life, and love in a little corner of New Mexico with me. I want to support her, but I want to remember this moment, too, with something I can hold and look at.

The crosses cover every square inch of available wall space, and my attention lands on a wooden one, painted in black and covered with dozens of tiny tin charms. The folk charms—in shapes of the flaming heart of Christ, flowers, babies, arms, kneeling figures, and even animals—are hammered all over the cross with equally tiny nails and painted gold. Anywhere my sight lands on the cross is a representation of something spiritual. I take the cross off the wall and turn it over. A small "Made in Mexico" sticker is stuck on the back announcing a modest price. It's perfect. I take it to the counter, which the customer has just vacated.

"I'd like to buy this one." The owner begins to pull pretty sheets of teal and brown tissue paper from a large roll on the wall and wraps the cross. She doesn't look at the price on the back.

"Why did you pick this one?" she asks. It's not a question I was expecting, but then again, the best things have always happened when I least expect them, and this day is a perfect example.

"I like that it's covered in all these charms," I say. I don't know what they are or what they mean, but I will learn.

"Yes, *milagros*. These all mean something unique. Good for prayers. Whenever you look at this," she says, holding up the wrapped cross, "just contemplate on what you're seeing." I learn later that she means for me to linger on a particular *milagro*, think about its spiritual purpose, and pray for that need or give thanks. I need prayers, and unbeknownst to me I have chosen a cross that is covered in petitions.

She drops the cross into a bag with her card. "For you!" she sings.

My wallet is in my hand, and it's my turn for my eyes to

widen. "Oh, no. I want to pay for this." She has given me so much through her conversation, kindness, and generosity of time, a precious gift that I know I cannot repay, and I want to give her *something* in return.

"Absolutely not," she says. I freeze for a moment, unsure of how to accept such a gift. I have asked to see Mary in this place, but I suddenly realize how short my faith fell. I expected I would just be reminded of her—and I have been—but I have received so much more from a stranger who clearly loves Mary, too. She has given me her attention, comfort, conversation, guidance, encouragement, friendship, and even shared tears. And now I am being given something physical, too.

It hits me we are no longer strangers, this owner and I. I finally relent and take the bag she holds extended from her hand.

"Thank you," I breathe. She comes around the counter and hugs me, and we laugh.

"I'll be praying for you," she says. "*Ev-ery-thing* is going to be all right. I know this to be true." She waves her hand in the air once again.

I know it will be true, too.

❈ THREE ❈

Prayers

> *And so from the outset prayer is really our humble ascent towards God, a moment when we turn Godwards, shy of coming near.*
> —METROPOLITAN ANTHONY OF SOUROZH[11]

IN MY SEARCH FOR Mary, I start small and try to echo what the shopkeeper last said to me: "I'll be praying for you." So, I begin very early in the morning to walk and pray.

For years my sleep has been poor. Deep in dreaming, I'm disrupted by some unimportant thought or half-forgotten anxiety from the workday at three or four AM. No matter how hard I try to shake it off, my brain clicks into processing, and I can't drift back to sleep. Exercise, to-do lists before bed, chucking the clock into the other room, caffeine sabbaticals—none of it seems to keep me asleep throughout the night. Recently I've stopped fighting it. If this is the pattern etched in my brain, I figure I'll work with it. I'll make the time spent tossing in frustration useful. I'll get up and pray.

The problem I find, however, is that I'm barely functional praying in front of our icon corner at this early hour. I sway, my eyes closed, and forget where I am in my prayers. Forty-five minutes pass, and I realize I've not remembered anything. I want to remember, to be able to contemplate the words, not to fall asleep standing up. So I start walking and praying instead.

The air is cool and light as I step onto the sidewalk lining our street this very early morning. It is a reprieve from the punishing heat of the early-summer day. Above, the moon winks into a silvery, half-closed eye, mimicking what everyone else is doing now, and a smattering of stars sparkle across the sky. Everything is perfectly quiet and still. Not even the puppies in the yard across our street stir at the sound of my tennis shoes steadily hitting the pavement.

I loop my long black prayer rope, a tool to help me repeat the Jesus Prayer, into my left hand and carry a travel mug of coffee in the other. It's an atypical combination, I know, to walk, pray, and sip coffee like this, but it works for me. I match the steady movement of my legs with my breath so I can walk and breathe in time with the words.

Lord, Jesus Christ, Son of God. I breathe in. Three steps.

Have mercy on me, a sinner. Exhale. Three more steps.

I advance a knot on my rope with my fingernail and press down, feeling the solidness of the next knot with the firmness of the ground beneath me. At the same time, I note the softness of the knot's black yarn surface. It feels the same as this black, gentled air of the night. Out here, walking along the sidewalks of my neighborhood, it is very dark, but the streetlights cast an orange glow through lines of live oak and maple, just enough light to see a few yards ahead of me. I sip my coffee, the energizing warmth spurring my heartbeat and raising my awareness of the night to all the details around me that merge with my prayer.

I walk and breathe, pray and sip. Whatever anxiety has

awakened me at this early hour loosens. I love walking at night. It feels secret and sacred, this quiet hour when no one is awake except me and maybe a few night creatures, hidden in the shadows of the alleys. I curve around a house's corner, a spot I know like the back of my hand after walking this same route for years during the day, and feel the earth begin to descend just a little toward the park in my neighborhood. As the streetlights recede behind me, what remains of the waning moon takes over as a heavenly lantern, barely lighting my way. Soon, I reach the park with its wide sheets of summer-green grass encircling two playa lakes.

Playas are the shallow pools of water scattered all over these southern plains. When it rains, runoff gathers in their depressions, creating temporary oases in the desert and recharging valuable underground water tables. From the air, playas resemble shimmering plates scattered all over the red mesas. They are vitally important in a landscape with no rivers or creeks. When a season is bone dry, they shrink and evaporate into chalky, gypsum bowls of cracked earth. However, when they are full, playas are home to all manner of wildlife: big, lumbering box turtles that emerge during summer rains, emerald-and-gray mallards, and sweeping flocks of migrating Canada geese who overwinter here on their shores.

I cross the last residential street and step onto the finely graveled trail encircling the park, the scent of the nearby water hitting my nose. Its earthy smell mixes with the dry scent of summer dust clinging to crepe myrtle blossoms and a few pines. A few park lights dapple between the leaves of old willows and aspens lining the playa, and the city's midnight sprinklers shoot long arches across the grass. During the day this will be turf for children's soccer teams and family picnics. At this early hour, however, long before dawn, no one and nothing else is here. It is just me, the advancing of my fingers along my prayer rope, the steady beat of my feet hitting the trail, and the words I whisper to God.

The diminished light, the sharp smell of still water, and the sleepiness of the neighborhood reduce distraction, and I feel as if, finally, I am present.

"How do I pray to Mary?" I asked my priest when I returned from New Mexico. I missed her easy presence now that I was back in the flat, sun-faded miles of West Texas where there were no old Catholic village churches or quaint stores to explore. I had also been reading about her life in *Mary, Worthy of All Praise: Reflections on the Virgin Mary* by Fr. David Smith and wondered what it must be like to go on pilgrimage and actually see the places where Mary lived. Many years ago, my grandfather had gone to the Holy Land, and although he wasn't Orthodox, he'd had his own kind of pilgrimage to holy sites—many of which, shockingly, were quite dangerous to visit at the time. I wanted to do that, too, and thought that maybe Mary would be easier to access if I could go to her.

But my priest told me the story of Diveyevo Convent in Russia instead. According to him, in the nineteenth century, St. Seraphim of Sarov, *starets* (elder) of this convent, ministered to a group of nuns who lamented they couldn't go on pilgrimage to visit the holy places. Their convent was just too far away, and a trip like that wasn't possible. Saint Seraphim instructed the nuns to dig a ditch around their convent, plant flowers around it, and erect a wooden boardwalk allowing them to walk around the site. He then taught the nuns to pray: "Rejoice, O Virgin Theotokos, Mary, full of grace, the Lord is with you! Blessed are you among women, and blessed is the Fruit of your womb, for you have borne the Savior of our souls!" According to his instruction, every day the nuns walked and recited this prayer 150 times. Saint Seraphim told the nuns that for anyone who walked along that place and prayed to Mary 150 times a day, the site would become like Jerusalem.

It's a powerful story, for in constructing their canal and making the physical beautiful, the nuns sanctified the ground with their prayers to the Virgin Mary. They created their own holy land with their prayers, and over time the convent itself became a site of pilgrimage.

I love this story. I am so far from the Holy Land and from the possibility of ever being able to make a trip to Greece or Jerusalem to see the places where Christ walked, the apostles preached, or the Virgin Mary lived. I had thought that going to the places where Mary walked, lived, and died would help draw me closer to her, but I understand through this lesson that's not necessary.

"You don't need to go on pilgrimage anywhere," my priest tells me. "Your backyard is far enough."

So after I finish praying a rope of the Jesus Prayer, I switch to this prayer to Mary, and I walk around the playa again.

"Rejoice, O Virgin Theotokos," I pray quietly. "The Lord is with you." Somehow by acknowledging He is with Mary, I become entwined with that truth. He is with me this morning, too, I know.

I pass along the east side of the playa and look down into the water. Ducks cloaked in the murky color of night bob in pairs, asleep on the pond's surface, their sweet little heads tucked around into their wing feathers. They don't stir as I pass, perhaps knowing somewhere deep in their sleep that I am not a fox or a dog. I consider this a good sign of trust.

"Blessed are you among women," I continue. "And blessed is the fruit of your womb."

On my left, my path meets a long strip of grassy earth, which disappears down into another, smaller playa fed by a shallow but jagged ravine. A metal bridge only a few feet wide crosses the ravine and links into the back parking lot of a metal-sided gym. From the reedy weeds framing this playa's shore, a small gray-and-white cat watches me with big eyes. As I come closer, it darts along the playa's dark banks, distrusting my intentions. That's okay, though. The sun will be up in a few hours, and I know as the grass warms and the park begins to stir with families, fitness gurus, and retirees walking their dachshunds that the cat will dart across the field into the surrounding neighborhood, where I have seen it before.

I am not a nun, and I am so far from Diveyevo Convent. But in my own way, I try to sanctify this ground with my prayers as I walk, praying to Mary in the dark cool of the park.

"For you have borne the Savior of our souls."

※

THE SUMMER HEAT ARRIVES FULL force by midmorning now. It is only the end of May, but the sun, arching overhead in its dazzling power, bears down on everything with such oppression that the tender petals on my backyard roses begin to dry and curl before the buds can even fully open. The grass dries and withers, too, and I pull potted geraniums out of the sunlight and onto my back porch where they will have at least a fighting chance to survive. When the wind comes in from the northwest, blowing across thousands of miles of open plains, the effect is like standing in a convection oven; the wind desiccates everything it races across. Only a prickly pear cactus I bought at a yard sale and some hardy yellow lantana, its leaves as rough as sandpaper, seem to thrive in the temperature. There is no fighting heat like this in West Texas; you simply have to stand in awe of its potency and wait out the brutal summer months until reprieve comes again.

Yet amid all this heat, my husband and I have noticed a hole growing underneath the old shed in our backyard. Once only a small opening in the packed and weedy dirt of a neglected flowerbed, the hole has grown in size over the last week and seems to be a tunnel leading from our driveway under the shed and into our backyard. When we get on our hands and knees to look, we can't see anything.

However, our eight-year-old rescue dog, Lucy, is obsessed with this hole. Every time she runs into the backyard, she makes a beeline for the shed, shoving her soft brown nose underneath it and inhaling with the skill of a sommelier, as if she were testing the quality of a fine wine before tasting it. Every day, she runs the length of the shed in the backyard, sniffing and snorting, sometimes jumping back in surprise, as if she's almost discovered the secret—or the secret's discovered her. Clearly something is under there, but nothing ever emerges.

It's not unusual in our neighborhood to have backyard visitors. I've seen possums, with their squinty eyes and long tails, lumbering across our patio in the middle of the night, searching for food. And last year we entertained a wild cottontail, whom we affectionately named Hidey-Bunny, for several months. We found her hidden in the faded irises behind our fence, a tiny, balled thing so sweet and unreal that we slowly backed away, afraid she'd disappear. Over a period of months, we watched her grow and hop all around our backyard, sometimes in the early morning, sometimes at dusk, until the mystery that had brought her to us eventually took her away.

However, I doubt whatever is under the shed is a possum or a bunny. It's piqued Lucy's attention in such a way she almost trembles with energy to get outside each morning. Plus, whatever is there has the ability to really dig, as the hole has grown larger.

I forget about it until one Saturday afternoon when, returning from an errand, my husband calls out to me.

"Brandi! Come look at this!"

He's crouched on the driveway, looking underneath the shed into the same black hole we always see when we're coming and going. When I reach him, his eyes light up. "They're *foxes*."

"What?" I exclaim. I quickly crouch down, nearly bumping my head against his to get a glimpse. The hole is dark, and a small stream of warm, musky air—not quite as hot as the afternoon—wafts out along with the sound of soft whimpering and scratching. I'm trying to see what he sees, and I don't have to wait long. One, then two, then *three* tiny black noses emerge. They tumble over each other, these little black dots surrounded by a mottled fur, until one desperately curious kit pushes his entire head outside the hole to look at us.

I melt, and it has nothing to do with the heat.

His little face is perfect: two blue-gray eyes set in a tiny mask of striped white and gray fur. He sniffs at us and darts back underneath the shed, torn between his instinct to hide and, perhaps, his growling belly. I'm not sure where his mother is, but I know she must be close. Foxes live in our neighborhood, too, but they are creatures of the night. Smart and lithe, they emerge as rust-colored shadows down alleyways and side streets to explore and do foxy nighttime things. Occasionally a neighbor will complain about them climbing trees or lounging on a roof in the cool hours of the dawn. I love them because they are adaptable and full of personality and a necessary part of the ecosystem. The fact they remain hidden during the day makes our discovery extra-special.

The little kit's boldness encourages his brother and sister, and they begin to push their dark noses out from underneath the shed, too, although they aren't brave enough to fully emerge. I coo to them like a mother and hold out my hand to show them they can trust me, and the little bold kit inches toward me, perhaps yearning to connect with me the same way I yearn to connect with him. I pull out my phone, hoping to get a photo to document our meeting.

But something old and ancient that separated us when we lost Eden kicks in, and the little fox changes his mind before I can touch him. My camera clicks just as he darts back underneath the shed. In the photo, his eyes are as black and shining as obsidian, and he's focused on the tips of my fingers, as if there's something in my skin that's pulling him to me. It's a supernatural moment of simple regard, and my husband and I feel touched by it.

"Three little foxes," I say as we stand up and dust ourselves off. "Our own little holy trinity of wildlife."

We walk back inside shaking our heads at the magic of it.

Prayers

I DON'T FULLY UNDERSTAND IT yet, but just by my taking on the act of more purposeful and consistent prayer, something has been set into motion.

My morning rising, walking, and praying becomes a craving, associated not with the caffeine I take with me but with the need to be in the presence of God and to talk to Mary. The park is quiet and dark, and there I can think without the distractions I have at home, even in the early hours before I get ready for work. At the playa, alone with the heavy air and stars of night, I get lost in the rhythm of praying not only the Jesus Prayer and the prayer to Mary, but also a whole set of Orthodox morning prayers I have finally managed to memorize.

As I walk to the park, passing the black hole that has grown uneasily quiet in the days since we discovered the foxes, I remember my original intention and ask for help to be present. The goal is to be with God, but Mary is there to help me, too, and so I ask her specifically for help.

In her beautiful book *Mary as the Early Christians Knew Her*, Frederica Mathewes-Green gives a lovely and simple explanation for why we ask for the saints' prayers, and in particular for those of Mary: "She loves us. A person moved by love is a sure help in trouble, and will pour out what could not be won by bargaining or flattery. A child knows this about his mother, that her love is something strong, and is a good place to find shelter."[12] She writes specifically about one of the earliest prayers to Mary, scratched down "on a piece of papyrus that was small enough to carry through the day":

Under your
compassion

*we take refuge,
Theotokos; do not
overlook our prayers
in the midst of tribulation,
but deliver us
from danger,
O only pure,
only blessed one.*[13]

The prayer is about 1,750 years old, and a version of it has been in use in the Orthodox Church all this time. It's a lovely prayer with some astonishing qualities. "First is the expectation that Mary is still alive," writes Mathewes-Green, "and able to hear such a request. . . . The second shocking thing is the expectation that Mary's prayers are effective."[14]

Prayer flows two ways, I realize. There are my prayers and petitions rising up, and there are the prayers of others gone before me, surrounding me in "so great a cloud of witnesses," flowing down (Heb. 12:1).

Yet, my praying isn't always easy, for in trying to encounter God, I often encounter not Him, but two things that cause me distress: my own resistance and inability to pray, and in that resistance, my true self. "Throughout the day we are a succession of social personalities, sometimes unrecognisable to others or even to ourselves," Metropolitan Anthony Bloom writes in his book *Courage to Pray*. "And when the time comes to pray and we want to present ourselves to God we often feel lost because we . . . have no sense of our own true identity."[15]

How true—and frightening—this is. Sometimes I start to pray, and I get stuck, unable to get the words out because I don't know how to be in the presence of God or to ask for help from Mary. Or I get distracted, and suddenly I'm not praying at all, but thinking about the day ahead, my future worries, or worse, my past hurts. Before I know it, I've walked a half mile and realize I've not been praying at all. Instead, I've been focusing on everything else—everything that is *me* and not *Him*.

I look at the darkness of the playa before me, a far cry from the Diveyevo Convent. I wish I knew whether the nuns there had struggled with their own effort to pray. I think about the little fox who inched forward, craving some kind of connection, but darted back into the dark when he got scared. Sometimes I am like this in the presence of God and those gone before me. I dart inward again when I bump up against the uncertain or uncomfortable. "If we remembered that every encounter with God . . . is a judgment, a crisis, we would seek God both more whole-heartedly and more cautiously," Met. Anthony cautions. "An encounter is only true when the two persons meeting are true."[16]

I suspect that this process is only beginning to uncover the true me, and that the real encounter is going to be harder than I expected.

I also suspect Mary has something more to teach me about this.

❈ FOUR ❈
Vessels

When the Great Archangel saw you, O pure one, the living Bible of Christ sealed by the Spirit, he cried out to you: Hail! O Vessel of joy, through whom the curse of the first mother is loosed.
—FROM THE AKATHIST HYMN TO THE THEOTOKOS[17]

THE ALARM CLOCK GOES off at its early hour this morning, and after a night of restless tossing, I groan and bury my head in my pillow. My tired body competes with my to-do list, the unknown emails waiting for me in my inbox, and the issues needing my attention today. My first instinct is that I don't want to get up this morning and go to work. My second thought is to worry what the day may bring. Do I have enough to give to the people who will need me today? Will I be able to handle what comes my way? I don't know, so I hit snooze and wedge myself deeper into bed. It's eight minutes that won't be restful, I know. I just keep my eyes closed, dreading the moment I have to get up and go. Lucy, our sleeping buddy, concurs. She lets out a frustrated sigh with my movement and snuggles in tighter against me.

I want to be the kind of person who cheerfully greets each morning, no matter what energy level I have, but this isn't always the case. For almost ten years, I have worked with college students who have learning disabilities and I have helped develop their tutors, the young professionals who help my students learn to be successful on their own and hopefully graduate college with a degree. It is very rewarding work, but it's also emotionally taxing. Mine is a caring profession, and there are a lot of people who need help in any given day, including the staff and employees I manage, struggling students, and concerned parents. I admire the kinds of people who never seem to worry, who maintain an inner peace that isn't ruffled by frustrated customers, rude employees, or the physical demands of the job.

However, I tend to get stressed about these issues and pour myself into my work to the point of depletion, which is its own kind of pride—a sticky, messy sin that warps my attitude and inhibits me from fully loving others. I am trying to understand why and when I do this so I can be more patient and generous and learn to give thanks for everything, "a great ascetic discipline,"[18] even on hard days when the reward isn't so obvious.

But still, I'd like to stay in bed just this once.

The alarm goes off again, and I finally push the covers off and lurch to my feet in the dark. This day has been given to me for a reason, I remind myself, and I have work to do—work that God has given me for a purpose (although sometimes that purpose isn't so obvious). I don't want to be a tired, cranky mess when I walk into work, so I have started praying the Prayer of Met. Philaret of Moscow: "O Lord, grant me to greet the coming day in peace. Help me in all things to rely upon Your holy will. In every hour of the day, reveal Your will to me. Bless my dealings with all who surround me. Teach me to treat all that comes to me throughout the day with peace of soul and with the firm conviction that Your will governs all."[19]

The prayer is a good reminder to be kind, pliable, and most importantly, *receptive* to what the day will bring and to God's will in it. It reminds me to be a vessel that He can use.

In fact, I want to be receptive and not fearful. This is my problem, I realize as I turn on the shower. I'm often motivated by *fear* of what-may-be rather than by *faith* in what-may-be. I fear the unexpected. Worse, I worry I might handle something poorly and fail to give the best advice, resolution, and guidance in a situation. Conflict, difficult conversations, holding people accountable, and making tough decisions with confidence are difficult for my personality. I much prefer independent work, harmony, and fading into the background of conversations rather than being the person people have to listen to. However, in my job, these difficult tasks are exactly the more challenging duties I have.

Still, I often wonder if I'm up to the job that God has given me and sometimes *why* He has given it to me. Even after working in my role for ten years, I feel sometimes there'd be a hundred people better suited to what I do than *me*, and this doubt makes me want to keep my head under my pillow.

Wouldn't it be so much better if I could default to a confidence that no matter what happens at work, God's presence is in it and He will help me through it? And that He's chosen me for this moment, conversation, or interaction, whatever the reason? I wonder what would happen if my response to this doubt and uncertainty was a humble "Yes, Lord, Your will be done" instead of a hesitant "Um, are You sure?"

What would happen if I relied less on my own abilities to get me through the day and more on God—because I truly had faith in what my Maker and Benefactor could do, alone and through me?

Expressing faith in what-may-be instead of fear of what-may-be is where Mary teaches me a lot, for her confident yet humble *yes* to God is what has brought the entire earth to this moment.

※

HOW MANY TIMES DID MARY say yes to God?

Many. So many, in fact, that her quiet, patient, unshakable faith is the very reason I am writing these words. She participated wholly and fully with God and accepted His will in every step of her life. She was the ultimate vessel for His work, and it was her continuous *yes*, given in her obedient faith and love, that brought Christ, and thus our salvation, into the world.

The Orthodox have a saying about the meeting of our wills with God's will: We have to *cooperate* with God's grace. As Frederica Mathewes-Green writes, "God wants us to be wholehearted participants in his work . . . because he wants to be in communion with us. The whole universe is arranged for the very purpose of enabling creatures to encounter God."[20]

What a beautiful truth. *Everything* in the world, from the ocean tides, to "random" encounters with strangers, to even the breadth and length of the crosses we each must bear, is all arranged in such a way that we might encounter God. He has formed creation for us that we might meet Him. Life, therefore, isn't meant to be a battle of what we want pitted against what God wants, and He is *never* going to force His will, which is always loving, onto us. A god who created man to do what he wanted wouldn't be a loving or benevolent god at all; a god like that would be a puppetmaster and would have no reason to come down, become flesh, and suffer with us, much less save us. Our God, "the Lover of mankind," is always going to give us a choice in life—either to follow Him or to reject Him—and that choice will be either to our benefit or to our destruction.

"There's a mystery to the dynamics of all this, too," Mathewes-Green continues. "God is Life, too, so being with Him and in Him means doing something active: praying, working, cooperating. . . . St. Paul uses the concept of synergy. He told the Corinthians, 'We are God's *synergoi*,' fellow-workers cooperating in a dynamic, unfolding story."[21] When we cooperate with Him, even when it's hard and we don't understand what He's asking or why, we are acting in the same faith and love He so desperately wants to bestow upon us, if we'll only let Him. We become partners, active participants, in the story He's written.

This is exactly what Mary did. When the archangel Gabriel came to her after her betrothal to Joseph, he told her:

> *"Rejoice, highly favored one, the Lord is with you; blessed are you among women!" But when she saw him, she was troubled at his saying, and considered what manner of greeting this was. Then the angel said to her, "Do not be afraid, Mary, for you have found favor with God. And behold, you will conceive in your womb and bring forth a Son, and shall call his name Jesus. He will be great, and will be called the Son of the Highest; and the Lord God will give him the throne of His father David. And He will reign over the house of Jacob forever, and of His kingdom there will*

be no end." Then Mary said to the angel, "How can this be, since I do not know a man?" And the angel answered and said to her, "The Holy Spirit will come upon you, and the power of the Highest will overshadow you; therefore, also, that Holy One who is to be born will be called the Son of God. . . . For with God nothing will be impossible." Then Mary said, "Behold the maidservant of the Lord! Let it be to me according to your word." (Luke 1:28–38)

I read Mary's reaction closely here. She isn't afraid because Gabriel *appeared* to her, for there isn't the slightest hint of surprise that an angel was talking to her. The Gospel is very clear on that. This is because we know from Orthodox tradition that Mary was a deeply prayerful person. In *Behold Your Mother: A Reflection on the Virgin Mary*, Metropolitan Isaiah of Denver writes that from the time of her youth,

> *Mary proved to be most devout, spending much of her time in prayer. From the writings of the Protoevangelium [of James] and oral tradition, it was said that Mary conversed regularly with angels during the years she lived at the temple. Therefore, it was not at all surprising to her, soon after she was betrothed to Joseph and had moved to Nazareth, that the Archangel Gabriel appeared to her. She was not at all troubled to see Gabriel. She was troubled at what he said to her.*[22]

It is obvious that Mary was deeply connected to God and the spiritual realm on a level of communication and intimacy I can only guess at. Gabriel's exaltation is one that carries great weight, for in greeting her as the "highly favored one" and "blessed . . . among women," he is declaring her status as the most blessed woman of all time for being destined to be the Mother of God. I am fairly certain that if an angel came to visit me, I would not handle the moment with such calmness and grace.

However, Mary did. She wasn't afraid that Gabriel visited her; she wasn't even afraid to converse with him. Rather, she was troubled by the details of what he *said* to her.

In her response, Mary conveys one of her virtues that makes her a model for all Christians: true humility. "She was being called by God," continues Met. Isaiah. "Why would God pay attention to one who saw herself as the least of God's people? She was no one to be considered, especially by God. She had to be overwhelmed when the Archangel Gabriel informed her that she was to give birth to the Son of God Who would sit on the throne of his father David and that there would be no end to his kingdom."[23]

Her reply to Gabriel in this moment is one of complete purity and innocence. Instead of questioning his declaration, demanding to know answers, asking for "proof" of such a proclamation, or asking him to explain what made her so worthy, "her pure and humble reply," writes Met. Isaiah, was "'How can this be, since I do not know a man?'"[24] Mary was a virgin, betrothed to Joseph but not yet married, and Gabriel answers her question and explains exactly how it is to be: "The Holy Spirit will come upon you, and the power of the Highest will overshadow you; therefore, also, that Holy One who is to be born will be called the Son of God. . . . For with God nothing will be impossible" (Luke 1:35, 37).

Without questioning this (which surely would have prompted *many* questions from anyone else hearing such an answer), Mary, of her own free will, accepts what the angel tells her. Although she might not understand in this moment exactly how it will all come to be, or the heart-wrenching consequences being the Mother of Christ will have for her when she stands at the foot of the Cross, watching her Son sweating, bleeding, and dying in agony above her, she cooperates with God and fully and freely accepts the role of the Mother of God.

Mary provides the resounding *yes* whose effect reverberates down to this very day: "Let it be to me according to your word" (Luke 1:38).

And because of this, the whole world has been saved.

※

I THINK ABOUT THIS ON my drive into work. How many times have I cooperated with God's will and said yes to what He was asking me to do, without complaint or reassurance? When have I been willing to say yes although I didn't understand what it meant or was afraid of the discomfort, loss, or suffering such an answer might bring me?

Not enough, I know.

I think about other times I've groaned inwardly when I didn't want to do something, or found myself frustrated with a request or impatient with a conversation that seemed to be going nowhere. It is difficult to look at these everyday moments, so fleeting they seem almost negligible, and realize my own pride, self-importance, and selfishness. Had I approached these interactions with the same humble, *receptive* attitude as Mary, they might have been a blessing both to me and to the other person. These are moments I was receiving a message, too, perhaps by visiting angels, but I didn't listen. I missed my purpose in those interactions.

I missed my *yes*.

※

THE WORKDAY BRINGS ITS USUAL challenges. A parent, angry that her son is failing a course, sends a hateful email to one of my staff. A younger student worker oversteps her bounds and breaks an important policy. One of my students reveals he hasn't been attending class, thus jeopardizing his grade. In each of these instances, I try to slow down, listen, and better understand the other person's perspective, rather than jumping into action to defend or fix. Instead of fearing the problem and trying to eliminate it, I open myself up.

The parent, it turns out, is worried about her son's success and defaults to blaming our office, and I guide my staff member through a fair and respectful response.

The student worker thought she was trying to be helpful but needs more training on the policy. We communicate a plan for improvement and think about other ways to help other employees like her in this situation in the future.

My student reveals he missed a test, which led to shame and avoidance behaviors, so we talk about his root fears, how to communicate to his professor about his responsibility as a student, and ideas for getting back on track.

In each of these instances, my role isn't glamorous or easy, and my help isn't outwardly appreciated or valued. The mother remains angry, but I know my staff member has been supported. The student worker isn't immediately receptive, but I know that I've given her valuable guidance and we learned something from the experience as supervisors and trainers. And my student may not follow through and talk to his professor, but I at least know I've given him room for honest self-reflection and accountability.

I think about Mary, who also was never guaranteed a road map for *how* her Son would achieve all the things Gabriel mentioned, only that He would. "He will be great," was all the archangel told her, "and will be called the Son of the Highest . . . and of His kingdom there will be no end" (Luke 1:32–33).

And still she said yes. This is where her exemplary humility, generosity, and sacrifice came into play for our salvation. She did not yet know what horrific suffering her acceptance would bring her. "She bore the Benefactor, she brought Him forth, and it was up to her whether she would give Him over to the prophecies she had heard, or keep Him for Herself," Fr. David Smith writes. "It all depended on her will, on her decision. Did she love the world enough to give up her Son, or would she leave the place where the Archangel came to her and never speak to anyone of that day again?"[25]

Could I have made such a difficult decision? Could I participate in that synergy in the same way Mary did? I don't know. I am reminded that Mary could have said no. She could have said the cost of being unwedded and pregnant was too great, too risky, in ancient Jewish society. She could have doubted or scoffed at the angel's explanation. She also could have said yes in the moment and then changed her mind later as she grew to love her son more and more, as any mother would. At any point along the way on the difficult road to Golgotha, she could have chosen *not* to cooperate with God.

But if she had, she wouldn't be who she is, nor would she be the model for all Christians to follow. "So, the power of the Theotokos does not rest in physical or intellectual strength, in artistic ability or the loyalty of her followers," continues Fr. David. "Rather, her wealth is her lovingkindness, her will, her 'yes' to God. In this way, we all become like the Mother of God. . . . We become free when we say 'yes' to God as the Theotokos did, and when we decide to give our suffering, our hopes, even our very lives to Him for the sake of the world."[26]

To acquire this kind of lovingkindness and align my will with God's is the goal.

In the last five minutes of the day, I close out my email, power down my computer, and lean back in my chair. The light outside settles far in the west and makes the old buildings on campus cast long, cool shadows on the grass. Down the hall I hear students working on their homework and a boisterous laugh from one of my favorite colleagues. I stand up, sling my purse over my shoulder, and turn off the light. As I close my office door, one of my student employees, a hardworking girl who's grown in confidence and skills each semester she's worked here, walks by on her way out the door.

"Bye, Brandi. Have a great night! Will I see you tomorrow?"

"Yes," I reply. I smile. "I'll see you tomorrow."

Yes.

✽ FIVE ✽

Mothers

Come deliver us out of dangers, O pure Mother of God,
since thou art mother of deliverance, and of the peace which
doth surpass all human reasoning.
—FROM THE FIFTH ODE OF THE PARAKLESIS[27]

I MOVE THROUGH QUIET DARKNESS this September morning. Above me, the moon shines in a perfect half circle: a silver wafer half-dipped in black. Neptune, distant and cold with its pulsing blue light, hangs close to the moon's border this month, although I need binoculars to see it in the crowded night sky. Autumn is right around the corner, but the air this morning is still warm. I shrug off my light sweater and tie it around my waist. The sound of its *swish, swish* against my legs and the soft patter of my steps are all I hear as I walk and pray.

A few dozen yards ahead of me, I see something small quickly flicker through the shadows. A cat, perhaps. Our neighborhood is filled with an extended family of feral black-and-white cats. They sometimes watch me from porch steps with piercing green eyes or scramble over fences to avoid my approach.

A few seconds later, however, another shape darts beneath a cluster of trees, but this profile is off. Too large for a cat. Too lean for a raccoon. Too bushy for a possum. I pause for a few moments, trying to piece together what it could be. What would be out here with me in the dark, weaving among the gray shadows like that?

I start walking again, although more slowly, and focus my eyes on where I saw the movement. Suddenly, a third creature steps out from beneath the shadows and into the glow of a streetlight.

A little fox. As I draw closer, I realize I'm seeing *three* little foxes darting and jumping among the rocks, hawthorn, and red yucca of a neighboring yard. Their eyes are large and glistening, and their ears—white-tipped and as big as satellites—turn in my direction as I approach. Two scatter and recede back into the night, but a third—a bold little one with eyes like obsidian—sits down in the middle of the street and calmly watches me as I walk past on the sidewalk.

My holy trinity of wildlife.

※

IT CONTINUES LIKE THIS EVERY morning. Sometimes I will see all three foxes darting among the bushes and rocks or lounging in the grass with the feral cats. Other times, it's just the one little bold one who sits in the middle of the street— waiting for me, I like to think.

"Good morning, babies," I whisper as I meet them. Their curious faces and large ears are all that meet me in reply. But we get used to each other, these foxes and I, and often they trail a safe distance behind me as I walk to the playa. When I stop and turn around to see where they are, they disappear into neighboring yards or back into the shadows. It's only the little bold one who follows me almost all the way down the street, stopping only when I step onto the park's trail. There seems to be some invisible border he's not quite ready to cross. He sits in the road behind me and watches me go until he disappears, evaporating into the blended shadows of night.

As I leave the foxes behind, the act tugs at my heart. I never know which morning I will see them, or if I will see them again at all, and the longing pulls at me. I begin to think of them as *my* little foxes and want to protect them as a mother would, but I know there is very little I can do. They are as untouchable as a distant galaxy, and I can only watch them from afar and give thanks for such a supernatural meeting. It's a supremely sacred gift.

I cross the street and enter the park. Just as my feet hit the trail's stone, my familiar prayer to Mary springs to my lips, as if it is not a prayer at all, but a heartfelt greeting for a beloved family member I'm meeting just ahead.

I sense she is waiting for me, expectant. I am alone on this morning as I always am, but not lonely. A feeling of tenderness rushes through me and presses on my heart, and it both comforts and confuses me. I pass across earth with nothing but inky sky and a few obscuring clouds above, and yet a palpable tenderness hems me in before I can even begin my prayers. This is the tenderness of a mother I am feeling, a sensation for which I have been longing. It is difficult because, although my mother lives with my husband and me, our relationship is strained, and I don't know how to undo the shame and guilt associated with that truth.

I have been coming to the Mother of God, I realize, longing for my own mother and the possibility of motherhood in my life. As I think about this, I pray "Most Holy Theotokos, save us," envisioning the wild foxes I've left behind, my own difficult relationship, and all the mothers and daughters I know. This is a prayer we repeat often during the Divine Liturgy and other services. It is often misunderstood as a statement that Mary is a co-savior with Christ and has the same saving power as God. However, "nothing could be further from the truth," as Stanley Harakas writes in *The Orthodox Church: 455 Questions and Answers*. "Christ is the only Savior and the only saving mediator between God and humanity."[28] Asking Mary to "save us" is asking for her help and intercession "before God's throne so that *He* may save us" (my emphasis).[29]

"Do you think," my priest asked me long ago when, as an early convert, I brought up the question of praying to Mary, "if you were walking along a river and suddenly saw someone drowning in the water, shouting, 'Save me! Save me!' that it would be wrong to stop and help because only God saves?"

"Of course not," I said. "I would stop and help."

"It's the same thing," he said, looking at me. "We aren't denying that God saves, but we are asking for help from others along the way. We are crying out because we need help. It's the same reason we ask our families and friends to pray for us. If the living can do that for us, why not the saints, angels, and Mary, who we know are already in God's presence?"

"One of the most humble acts we can perform," writes Fr. David Smith, "is to sing the words, 'Most Holy Theotokos, save us!' and embrace the total reliance on God that these words express."[30] It is extremely humbling to cry out in need to a person in this way, especially to the Mother of God. But as James wrote, "The effective, fervent prayer of a righteous man avails much" (James 5:16). Mary is undoubtedly righteous, and I have no doubt her prayer is effective and fervent.

I recite the prayer to her again as I walk: "Most Holy Theotokos, save us."

The words fall as quickly as stars in the night sky.

※

THE TERM *THEOTOKOS* IS UNIQUE to Orthodox Christianity. It means, literally, "God-bearer," for Mary bore God in her womb. The term "summarizes," as Harry Boosalis writes in his book *Person to Person: The Orthodox Understanding of Human Nature*, "our belief that Christ is truly God and truly human."[31] The earliest Christians in the Church so fervently debated this title and its use that it took the Third Ecumenical Council in Ephesus in 431 to confirm its place in theology. Bishop Nestorius in Constantinople, for example, believed that Mary should be called *Christotokos*, or "Christ-bearer." However, such a term, argued others such as St. Cyril of Alexandria, undermined the very essence of Christ.

As Boosalis writes, "The title Theotokos is above all a Christological term expressing, in one word, the Orthodox Church's teaching on the full and complete divinity, as well as the full and complete humanity, of our Lord Jesus Christ."[32] If one believes that Christ is, in fact, God, then it follows that Mary was His Mother, which points out another facet of this term: "It should be obvious that when [the Third Ecumenical Council] adopted the title *Theotokos*, they did not think it meant that Mary conceived the Trinity," writes Mathewes-Green, "or that she existed before God the Father.

. . . This title for Mary is primarily a statement about Jesus. It is designed to emphasize his divinity from the moment of conception."[33]

Saint Cyril won, and the Nestorian controversy, as we now know it, died away.

It is no small thing to recognize I am making a conscious effort to meet and understand the woman who bore the very God of the universe, the Creator of all these mysteries. What kind of mother, then, was she?

BACK HOME, I KICK OFF my sneakers and pass by the wall calendar on which a particularly painful note is etched in my mother's handwriting: "My heart died with his and I'm just leftover, waiting for heaven. That's LOVE."

It's scrawled on September 20, the anniversary of my father's death, and it's there because I provoked the point I always make when it comes to my mother's grief: I am alive, and my father is not.

My father has been dead for nine years, and for nine years, his death has been the axis, as far as my own flawed perspective can understand, on which my relationship with my mother has turned. After he died unexpectedly from heart complications, my mother struggled as she suffered in her overwhelming grief. Everything that was once "normal"—work, routine, relationships—dissipated in the unexpected shock of his passing, including, at times, her will to live. Over time, her grief took on a life of its own, warping everything with its gravity.

Within a year of my father's passing, my parents' home went into foreclosure. The news came too late to my husband

and me, despite repeated requests for information and the opportunity to help. Somehow, we were always two steps behind and left out of major decisions.

After her home was sold, moving became my mother's search for happiness and mimicked the constant moves we made through most of my childhood, from small town to small town. We never settled anywhere for long, and during an astonishing six years we lived in the same town, we moved houses three times.

Following the sale of my parents' home, my mother changed addresses as often as she could, sometimes every six months. She moved from rental house to apartments and back in our town, trying to find the perfect spot that would make her happy. With each move, my gut clenched. I wanted nothing more than for my mother to be settled and somehow frame a new life and rhythm of her own without my father. What other choice was there, I thought in the moments when it was too hard to process my own pain, but for our lives to go on?

But as time passed, my mother's grief swelled like a summer storm and covered everything in a deluge of anger, sadness, and despair—most of that, it felt, directed at me. Somewhere along the way, her anger found its way to my mailbox. She wrote me long letters filled with her pain and subsequent disappointment in me. How I was failing her as a daughter, how I wasn't doing the things she felt an only daughter should do in such a time. The underlying message was that it was my job to alleviate her sadness and make her feel better. The letters also held hints of jealousy and resentments.

"You're married, and I'm not," she wrote in one. "And I don't have anyone."

I know that this came from a place of incredible pain and loneliness, but I was hurting, too. "I'm not your friend!" I finally exploded at her over the phone one day when another letter listing everything I wasn't doing arrived at my door. "I'm not Papa's replacement or a person you can dump on. I'm your daughter, and I've lost my dad!" The unspoken expectation didn't feel fair: that I bear the brunt of my mother's sadness and also fill the void that my father left. I tried to explain what I needed and how we processed our grief differently, but silence reigned on the other end of the line.

"I just can't be angry all the time, Mama." I relented.

"But you're supposed to talk to me. You're my daughter."

I didn't disagree. My mother's family was one of storytellers and laughter, often hiding, I learned later in life, deep wounds of family abuse, neglect, and dysfunction. Despite that, before my grandmother died when I was ten, every family gathering involved lots and lots of talking. On the porch. Over the phone. At tables spread with homegrown onions, cornbread, and pots of boiled beans. They talked about each other, too, retelling stories I learned by heart. I loved to listen to the raucous cacophony of them, now long gone.

But my introverted tendencies baffled my mother. Where my mother's grief burned like the sun, hot and vivid, mine quietly smoldered within my heart. I learned to process in private, through writing, in time at church, or with my husband, who had also lost a parent. "Talking" to my mom really meant listening to her talk, complain, or, sometimes, cry. I could do that; in fact, I knew I was being called to do that, as best I could. But I could only listen for so long, for she never asked me how I was doing or what I needed. I felt like a receptacle into which she could pour her bitterness, and when I didn't respond the way she wanted, she got angrier, more disappointed. And I retreated more.

Eventually, my mother and I became two planets caught in each other's oblong orbit, pushed and pulled by the force of what we wanted from each other but somehow couldn't achieve.

"But I am still alive!" I told her more than once when I tried to make her understand how I felt. I wanted her to acknowledge my pain and to be grateful that I was still here, even though my father was not.

"But I'm not alive anymore," she returned. "My heart died with Papa." The words echoed like an empty room in an abandoned home.

※

I PAUSE BY THE NOTE again, a few contorted words filled with so much anguish. They are scribbled on my calendar because despite these difficult years, I want my mom to be happy and well, and my husband wants to make sure that no matter what happens, we can look back and say that we did what we could, that we helped in the most selfless way we could think of. This is why we've invited my mother, who was struggling to live on her own, to live with us instead.

It is so much harder than I anticipated. Living with us seems to have made things worse and not better. The latest letter from my mom, which I find on my counter one evening after a long day at work, is four pages of vitriol. We have gone into debt moving my mother into our house, including taking on a car payment so that she can have reliable transportation and covering a myriad of expenses to get her account into the black. My husband hunted down her pawned wedding rings, her only valuables, and bought them back.

None of this really matters, though. I can't even pinpoint what triggered this latest letter, but I sit patiently and read it, numb now to the anguished stream of consciousness that zags across the page. I sigh and fold it up.

All I can really do now is pray. I pray for softness and the release of anger. I pray for patience and for understanding of her pain and perspective. I also pray for healing, to be unconsumed by past hurts, and to forgive both her and myself.

Lastly, I pray to let go. A good portion of this experience has taught me about the unhealthy dysfunction that somehow surfaced in our relationship in the years since my dad died. Somewhere along the way, I really started to believe what she said—that I never did enough for her—and I started to feel guilty for everything. That I have a living husband. That I have a job. That I have maintained a home. That I have friends and a church family and hobbies to feed my body, mind, and spirit. All blessings, I know, that can be easily lost at any moment. But I have also felt guilty for finding a way to move forward, however difficult that might be at times, when it seems that my mother cannot.

I foster a strong concern for her immediate needs, which I am providing, but I pray to care a little bit less about what she has written and not always believe that I'm somehow failing her all the time. I'm tired by that thinking, and so I pray, mostly to Mary, and ask to be delivered.

All I want now are two things: peace in my heart, which is like learning a second language, and peace in my home. "Come deliver us out of dangers, O pure Mother of God, since thou art the mother of deliverance, and of the peace which doth surpass all human reasoning," implores the Fifth Ode of the Paraklesis (a collection of eight odes of praise and supplication honoring Mary).[34]

"Help deliver us," I pray.

And that inexplicable tenderness meets me as I walk into my bathroom and start to get ready for work. It sets me on a crying jag because at thirty-eight, I still want to be comforted by a mother, and somehow a mother is here. She gave birth to God manifest in the world, to Jesus Christ who promised in His Sermon on the Mount that the mourners would be comforted and the peacemakers would be called "the sons of God" (Matthew 5:4, 9). Mary reminds me, in her unfailing example, to have patience and compassion with this situation, just as she has compassion on the entire world.

That's love.

❋ SIX ❋

Holding Lightly

> *Then I heard her voice, full of fragrance and sweeter than honey, saying to me, "Did I not tell you to place your hope in me? Why are you disheartened? Here, take Christ!"*
> —ELDER JOSEPH THE HESYCHAST[35]

THIS EVENING AFTER WORK, I decide to take a quick walk around the playa. The air outside, laden with early-autumn smells of mesquite and drying bark, sinks coolly onto my skin as I walk. At the playa, children scream and laugh as they play soccer in the grass. I hear their little voices, bouncing off the houses across the street and making them seem bigger than they are, before I even arrive at the water. This evening the horizon is all yellow and gray, and the sunset bounces across silvery water like a stone of light.

The random assortment of life here is different at the end of the day than at the beginning. People I've never seen before in my neighborhood wash in with the after-school hours and wash back out with the waning of the light. Only I remain after the sun sinks beneath the horizon. I watch them leave for their homes and bedtime routines as I walk.

A father, still dressed in business casual, walks ahead of me and shouts to his son not to stay behind too long. The son shouts back that he won't. The boy whizzes by me on his bright yellow bike with two of his friends, their voices high and chirping like sparrows.

It is late October, and the days hang tenuously on the edge of change. Already I can see tufts of orange leaves peeking from the highest branches of the trees like petticoats of a Halloween costume, the hue echoing in the lines of pumpkins, gourds, and toothy decorations already spilling across the porches of my street. Soon the West Texas evenings will be blissfully cool, and sunsets of magenta, orange, and buttercup will color the skies over dried cornfields.

Amidst the anticipation, another change hangs in the air, but this one is hard for me. For a long time, I've clung fiercely to a belief that living with us would be The Best Thing for my mom and that my home would bring her healing and peace. However, I was terribly wrong. Almost from the start, it has been a disaster, her expectations crashing against mine until anger and resentment built up to the point where she violated a hard line of trust. As a result, I have asked her to move out. It grieves me, for I've realized what I want for her and what she wants for herself are two completely different things. I thought I could control—or at least influence—what she did next in life and ensure she'd be in a safe, free living situation, but that isn't what she wanted. She wanted an experience I just couldn't give her, and that makes me feel like a failure.

"We are just too different," she wrote in another note she left for me to find when I got home from work. Accepting that we are different is not hard; accepting that we are "too different" to live together and that my mother is stepping back into another period of uncertainty after my husband and I worked so hard to provide her with stability is another matter. While she is under my roof, I feel relief because I know she is safe, and I don't have to worry so much about her.

But at the same time, she's been miserable, which in turn has made our home as cold as the breeze skimming across the water this evening. I see now that I can no more control the outcome of my mother's life than I can control these trees above my head holding onto their leaves. I wanted to ensure that one parent would be okay. I thought what I could provide was enough, but I was wrong. A new season is coming for our family, whether we like it or not.

Still, the rejection hurts, and I am afraid of what the future holds for my mother.

"But she's going to die!" I sobbed to my priest late one evening when my husband and I were discussing with him what to do. It was really a conversation about how to let her go, accept her free will, and maintain boundaries that wouldn't tear our home apart.

"Brandi," he said, his voice calm but authoritative. "Of course she's going to die. We're all going to die." *You can't keep her from dying*, he implied.

Behind him, a full moon rose in the dark rectangle of his office window. I could grasp at that moon forever, every night of my life, but I'd never be able to stop its movement or keep it from phasing into blackness.

The same is true for my mother. My father's death was so unexpected and resulted in so much grief that I thought living with us would be a way to prevent that happening with her. But I am totally powerless to prevent death or suffering from happening in her life, no matter how hard I try, how tightly I grip. I have to let that unrealistic belief go. I also have to let *her* go and make the decisions she ultimately wants to make, whatever their outcomes.

In Orthodox icons of Mary, the Theotokos always holds her Son lightly. She is never clutching Him, pressing Him against her breast to shield Him from the world. She holds Him as one would hold something beautiful and delicate, always aware that crushing Him to her in fear or protection would inhibit His ultimate purpose.

Mary felt the pain all mothers feel when their children grow up, and she was warned of the impending doom of the grief and pain that would pierce her very soul as she watched Christ die on the Cross: "Then Simeon blessed them, and said to Mary His mother, 'Behold, this Child is destined for the fall and rising of many in Israel, and for a sign which will be spoken against (*yes, a sword will pierce through your own soul also*), that the thoughts of many hearts may be revealed'" (Luke 2:34–35, emphasis mine).

Orthodox icons always teach the theology that it is ultimately not about what Mary wanted as a human mother, which was, no doubt, to protect her Child against everything she possibly could, fueled by her powerful and bone-crushing love.

She already knew, however, from this prophecy, that she could not.

Instead, in Orthodox icons she holds Him lightly, always turning Him toward the viewer. She presents Him to the world, as if at any moment He might spring from her lap and go off to do what we all know He eventually does: go boldly into the world He loves so much to suffer and die for it. This is, in fact, why Mary is rarely featured alone in Orthodox icons and why our churches are not adorned with images or statues of her alone.

As Frederica Mathewes-Green writes, "When we see an image of Mary as a young woman holding her baby, or as a pregnant woman with the child visible in her womb, we may think, 'There's an icon of Mary.' But that's not quite right; it's really an icon of the Incarnation."[36] The Incarnation—the Word made flesh and its astounding implications—is, for Orthodox Christians, always the focus. Icons of Mary *always* direct us to Christ. "Such images are not general portraits of her," continues Mathewes-Green, "but depictions of a turning point in the history of salvation."[37] And because icons of Mary always point the way to Christ, she holds Him lightly, setting up that important theological foundation in tones of red, gold, and blue.

When I look at icons of Mary holding Christ, I am always struck by the precious strength and constraint with which she holds her Love. In my opinion, the prophecy of Simeon is both joyful and terrifying. Mary *knows* what is coming—a grief and pain like no other—and although she can no more constrict the will of God than she can hold back the sea, she chooses to work with that reality. She watched her precious Son grow in "wisdom and stature, and in favor with God and men" (Luke 2:52). She accompanied Christ on His preaching circuits. She witnessed His miracles. She watched Him being driven from towns by hatred and dying on a cross like a common criminal while everyone else who claimed to love Him fled. She felt the piercing of His side and His last breaths on the Cross as a sword through her own heart.

And all that time she held Him lightly, lightly. She never

clutched at Him or pulled Him back. She didn't orchestrate His life to prevent His pain or the consequences of His love. How could she? She was not God. Instead, she patiently served, loved, and followed Him, all the way to Golgotha.

My life is nowhere near the same as Mary's, but what this teaches me! How much of her example I can model in my own life and learn to hold onto lightly, knowing full well I have to let it go for God's full will to be done.

A breeze picks up across the lake, and the leaves rustle.

The father, more distant now, calls to his boy again. Boy and bike whiz by me, blurring together into the last yellow light, chasing the father home.

※

BUT STILL, I STRUGGLE. THE next weekend, I walk back to the playa before the sun rises and try to sort out overwhelming feelings of fear and failure as I walk.

Fear of what I am humanly unable to do—somewhere along the road to this day I have taken upon myself responsibility for my mother's happiness and well-being. Failure because I can't possibly succeed.

I try to reason out where I picked up this unfair load: Was it in the disappointed letters she sent me over the years? The tears she cried relentlessly over my dad?

The fact that he is dead, and not me? It's a terrible thought and one I try not to entertain for long. I know my mom loves me, just as I love her. She just doesn't know how to engage that love, because if she did, it would mean she'd have to change, and change would mean letting go of the prison of grief to which she's consigned herself.

"You don't love me!" my mother said to me after I

approached her about her last note, the one in which she says we are "too different" to live together.

"Mama, of course, I do," I sighed, my head against the doorjamb of her room. "Otherwise I wouldn't have done all this." But she wants to see love exhibited in a different way—by giving her what she wants, requests that I can't fulfill in my home. I looked around her room, filled with photos of my dad, a memorial to his life and their marriage. There isn't a single photo of me anywhere.

Now my mother, at my request, is staying with a friend until she can sort out a new living arrangement. The room my husband and I painted purple—her favorite color—is mostly packed, but I work to box up what is left lying around. Clothes, CDs, and family mementos are scattered across the space.

In her closet, on top of an open trinket box, I find a black-and-white photo my husband took of my dad and me when I was in graduate school. In the photo, I am kneeling beside my father as he sits in a chair. I look so young, and my dad looks peaceful and at ease. We smile into the camera. On the back, my mother scribbled, "I don't like b/w pictures. Brandi was young at heart then. Papa was happy . . . The way life was supposed to be. Boy, did I get screwed!"

I know this is the cry of a person in pain and deep depression, a cry from someone who sees her life as not turning out at all the way she thought it should have. I know when she pulled the photo out of its hour-processing envelope she scribbled those words in anger. I have compassion on the person who wrote her thoughts so violently they almost bleed. But still, to find the photo left in the open hurts.

The haunting thought returns: I am alive, and my dad is not. I let the photo flutter to the floor.

Asking my mom to move out is the hardest, most difficult decision I have ever made. My husband and I debated the decision at length. We sought spiritual counsel, as well as advice from trusted friends, family members, and counselors.

"What else do you want her to do?" my priest gently asked me that night as the moon rose in his window. "Do you want her to destroy you? You have to let people live their lives, Brandi," he said. "And that means letting them live with the consequences of their choices. We always knew this might be temporary."

I knew he was right. From the very beginning, his counsel about our decision to let my mom live with us included the observation that my mom might not be happy, and given her restlessness, might move right back out. After all the money and effort my husband and I expended, we couldn't imagine such an outcome in less than a year. We were prepared to have her live with us forever. I had visions that a free, comfortable place to live with access to food and other necessities might mean my mom would cook again, or work an easier part-time job, or delve into a new routine unburdened by the previous living arrangements she couldn't manage.

But I was wrong, and my priest's prediction was true.

And now I feel that by maintaining a boundary of peace and trust in my home I am forcing consequences to happen.

I think about all of this as I walk this morning and find myself leaving the trail. I cut across the grass to a line of birch trees along the water, sink down against the solid wood, and begin to cry. I pray to Mary for my mom and for myself and for all the disappointments that seem to stack like blown branches from the trees around me. I pray for what is bigger than me, for what I must accept, and again, for what I must let go. My prayer is muddled and confused, no intelligible words taking shape, until finally a litany emerges that I time with my breath: *Most Holy Theotokos, take care of my mom.*

I suppose they are really the most holy words I can utter.

For a long time, I sit and sniffle against my sleeve, not knowing what else to do. The morning is so clear and bright that it's like looking through glass. If anyone were walking in the park this morning, I wouldn't see them, so utterly blinding is the rising sun, burning away all the shadows of the night.

Just then, I look down through my blurred vision and see it.

Filaments of glittering silk. Thousands and thousands of tiny filaments, connecting each blade of grass. For as far as I can see from my angle on the hard, damp ground, the intricate web stretches out like a net, connecting every living leaf and creature, all the way to the water's edge, where the silk disappears. Some tiny, unseen host of spiders has woven a web of light all over the grass.

It is all so beautiful: the golden light streaming through the trees, the daylight caught in threads of diamond on the ordinary ground beneath me. I've sat down right in the middle of glittering light I never would have seen from the trail, and I had to be broken to see it. The thought halts my tears for a moment as I realize I am witnessing mercy.

"Why are you disheartened?" Mary once asked Elder Joseph the Hesychast when he began to despair.

These words jump into my head as I sit on the banks of the playa, my sacred ground. The smallest breeze moves over the grass, and the filaments shimmer and shake, turning light into straining strands that don't break. A down feather, wrestled from above, sinks through the air in front of me. I hold out my hand and catch it before it falls into the web. I blow it away from my palm, out into the morning where it can drift again on the wind. Out toward the world and the water, where it is free.

❧ SEVEN ❧

Dryness

> *Weakness . . . means being completely supple, completely
> transparent, completely abandoned in the hands of God.
> We usually try to be strong and we prevent God from
> manifesting His power.*
> —METROPOLITAN ANTHONY BLOOM[38]

It is November now, and at last autumn has released its green hold on the fields. The first bitter winds sweep over the plains, and an early darkness descends in late afternoon. Weeks of work travel, end-of-semester fatigue, and the cold weather have kept me inside, and I can't seem to rise at my normal early hour. I lie in bed longer as the darkness presses heavily, dreaming forgettable dreams before waking, wondering about my trio of foxes slipping through the cold night air before I fall back asleep.

I do not walk and pray these mornings. I have let the habit of staying in bed longer usurp my old routine. Instead, when I finally get up, I stand in front of our icon table, rubbing my eyes and swaying with sleep. With the end of the year approaching, everything feels heavier and harder. In front of the icons, I light candles and incense and begin to pray, but this effort, too, is heavy. I feel none of the warmth or presence I felt before.

Outside, the driving autumn winds whip the tree branches, still laden with turning leaves, but bring no rain. We are entering our dry winter season, which brings with it months of cold and biting air, but very little snow or rain. It's a period that strips everything bare, including skin and spirit, if one is not careful.

My prayers this morning feel dry, too, devoid of emotion or even conviction.

I say them anyway. The words seem brittle as they fall from my lips, the same as the dead leaves just beginning to pile outside the door.

※

ONE WEEKEND I WALK TO the playa. The sudden cold weather has shot through the trees, shocking them into brighter colors, like the cheeks of children still playing in the grass. I walk by a shadowed trio of afghan pines, the ground littered with bursting cones. They have given up their summer secrets and succumb to a death on the ground. On the other side of the pines the eastern sunrise crests farther south on the horizon.

Other trees around the playa have begun to relent, too. The desert willow and crepe myrtle are already bare, their brown leaves scattered across a field. I walk along the path and crunch over fallen acorns of live oaks, whose color release begins at the top of their crowns in bright halos. To the path at my right, an ebony tree spirals spindly pods from its branches, also going bare. But near the water, bald cypresses have turned fire-orange, the fingers of their long leaves still reaching toward the sky, and one globe willow still breathes its roundness. For now.

I am sad and anxious these days for several reasons. Usually the end of the year and its holidays bring me joy, but this year I feel a keen sense of time's uncontrollable passage, and with it, my powerlessness over its pace. This year slipped by so quickly, and the holidays feel like they are arriving too soon. The Nativity Fast will soon begin, and I don't feel prepared for it or for the ensuing celebration we'll have at the end of the year. My mother is safely settled into a new living arrangement, but the wounds of that transition are still sore. But most of all, for the first time ever, I feel my age and what remains unaccomplished, for my husband and I want to have a baby.

Our married life took unpredictable turns that prevented us from focusing on a family early on. But now we have entered a season bright with clarity in which we know with absolute certainty we could be good parents. By the grace of God, we are healthy and healing from life's wounds. It's been like stepping from a heavy, dark wood into a bright and open clearing where the horizon of what's possible can be seen for the first time. We both believe that God paved a way through these struggles for us to arrive at this place, and that He's prepared us through everything to be parents. Something within me has also been ticking, like a clock winding down, making me acutely aware of all this year has brought—both blessings and lessons—and what might be possible moving forward.

However, a trip to my doctor revealed having a baby might not be so easy. I am apparently of "advanced maternal age" since I am over thirty-five. I was rejected for services by a recommended OB/GYN and instead I was sent to a fertility specialist, whom I can't see for another year due to her busy schedule. I don't even know if I have fertility problems, but the automatic assumption by doctors I haven't even met has left me feeling bereft, fearful, and worst of all, as if I have missed something in a way I could have prevented. It's a terrible feeling.

My husband and I talk about what we can do, and he reminds me that this is *truly* a place where we must trust God and let Him work. I know this, but sometimes cold fear swirls inside me like the leaves in the wind. I think about all the sweet and beautiful children in our church and the way my husband lights up around babies, and I'm filled with a sudden longing that is wonderful and terrifying all at the same time. What if I can't get pregnant? What if, after all this time, we won't be able to have a baby after all? The worry of this presses so heavily on me this morning I don't know what to do, so I walk beneath the shedding trees. The morning light dances so easily through nearly naked branches that sky is visible more than tree. I feel a similar exposure. I pray to God, the Creator of all things, but I feel an absence, as open and silent as the blue above me.

My heart feels like it's about to break, and I ask for help again.

Help not just for our desire for a family, but for the dryness of spirit that has descended on me in recent weeks and left me feeling empty and brittle. Help for my lack of faith and trust in God's will. Help for the sudden fear and helplessness by which I am gripped and the egoistic belief that I am in control of anything.

Help me with this, I pray to Mary. *Help me to let go of this worry and trust.*

I keep walking.

※

THERE IS A BEAUTIFUL SERIES of thirteen prayers to the Theotokos, simply titled "Prayers to the Theotokos," that have long been beloved and prayed in the Orthodox tradition. Often incorrectly attributed to St. Ephraim the Syrian, an early Church Father, they were actually "written in Greek by patristic and Byzantine writers, whose names for the most part have been lost or were never recorded," writes Archimandrite Maximos Constas in the introduction to *Mother of the Light: Prayers to the Theotokos*.[39] The series focuses intensely on a "profound spirit of contrition, compunction, sorrow for sins, and the desire for repentance," for the writers were acutely aware of the self-imposed suffering that distance from God creates and longed for forgiveness and unification again.

This longing is what I have felt lately. Only a few months ago, prayer felt as easy and free-flowing as water and was the most comfortable of conversations. But lately, something has shifted within me, brought on by a self-imposed distance I created from habit, worry, and focus on everything *except* God.

As I reread *Beginning to Pray*, I am struck by a subject that Met. Anthony discusses in detail: the absence of God in our life. "Obviously," he writes, "I am not speaking of a real absence—God is never really absent—but of the *sense* of absence which we have. We stand before God and we shout into an empty sky, out of which there is no reply. . . . What ought we to think of this situation?"[40]

Dryness

He goes on to explain that "prayer is an encounter and a relationship" and something that cannot be forced by one of the parties in that relationship. It must be mutual. God is always present and available, but we so rarely make time for Him. "We complain that He does not make Himself present to us for the few minutes we reserve for Him," continues Bloom, "but what about the . . . hours during which God may be knocking at our door . . . or when we do not answer at all . . . or even hear the knock at the door of our heart?"[41]

I wonder, then, if there's been a knocking, and I've just missed it . . . or been unwilling to hear it. Have the answers to my problem of spiritual dryness and feelings of absence been as obvious as the bright blue sky shining outside between the tree limbs? Have I, perhaps, been the source of this problem after all?

I suspect that I have been.

I return to the thirteen Prayers to the Theotokos. The third prayer begins:

> *O Virgin Lady Theotokos, who carried Christ our God and Savior in your womb, I place all my hope in you, and it is in you, who are higher than all the angelic powers of heaven, that I trust. Protect me, O all-pure One, by your divine grace. Set my life on a straight course, and direct me to the will of your Son and our God. . . . As the Mother of God and Mistress of all creation, you are able to do this.*[42]

So much is packed into these brief few lines. Immediately, the undeniable power of Mary as an intercessor takes center stage. Because she is the one who carried God in her womb, she becomes the model of the Christian life and the motherly guide of all seeking her Son. She knows what it means to seek the will of God, as well as His presence. Who better to ask for help in that than her, who understands, as a human woman, what that means?

Reading the lines I am aware of how *needful* the author is and how much *help* is being requested. "Place . . . trust . . . protect . . . set . . . direct": the author is crying out to Mary to assist with action in what the writer is unable or not strong enough to do himself.

I recognize this needfulness in myself. Through sheer force of habit, discipline, or will, I cannot accomplish any measure of faith by myself, nor can I force a spiritual encounter or relationship. My prayers have been dry lately, I realize, because I had been relying on my effort alone to make them meaningful. Even in this, I must ask for help. Prayer III reminds me I cannot have hope or faith in myself. I can only have it in her Son, the Living God whom I ultimately seek through this relationship. It also reminds me—again—that Mary will help me with this.

Likewise, I cannot protect myself from what may or may not happen in my life, and in those situations, I cannot discern the will of God using my rationality alone; I must depend on God in total trust. I must acknowledge my weakness in these things and ask for help: help that is required to make anything possible.

In another section, the prayer continues:

> *This I ask knowing that you are the helper of the exhausted from their labors, the protector of all who are in danger, the savior of those who are lost, the safe harbor of those imperiled by the waves of life, and the strength and helper of those surrounded by troubles. Grant me, your servant, compunction, peace of mind, stability of intention, intelligence of*

> *mind, vigilance of soul, a humble spirit, a peaceful and holy disposition, and a wise and controlled demeanor, for these are things which reveal the inner, peaceful condition and good order of the soul that the Lord promised to give his disciples.*[43]

Everything I have struggled with lately and desperately need pours out in these lines. The chaos of worry, created in fear, does indeed make me feel "lost" and "imperiled by the waves of life." I long for that peace, stability, vigilance, and good order which the prayer so aptly identifies and which the Lord promised to His disciples. I want to rest from the labors of my mind. The knowledge that I can ask this through Mary is a relief.

And some final lines in this prayer:

> *Tear up the catalog of my sins. Scatter the clouds of my sorrows, and dissolve the gloom of my troubled thoughts. Remove from me the tempest and turmoil of passions, and keep me in peace and tranquility. Open my heart that I might perceive spiritual things. Fill me with joy, exultation and gladness beyond words, so that I might hasten along the straight paths of the commandments of your Son, walking upon them with a clean conscience. . . . Grant me the gift of pure prayer . . . chanting with gratitude, praying with joyfulness of heart, and glorifying and honoring and praising your only-begotten Son, our Lord, Jesus Christ.*[44]

Gratitude. This is what I have been missing. In all my worry and overwhelm, I have forgotten St. Paul's admonition to "Rejoice always, pray without ceasing, [and] in everything give thanks; for this is the will of God in Christ Jesus for you" (1 Thess. 5:16–18). To give thanks for everything, *including* the dryness, struggle, and uncertainty, is to foster a mindset that wholly accepts God's will and positions me as subservient to Him. To be in submission to His will is to be small in His power. Yet there is great hope and strength in this, as well, for as Christ said, "My grace is sufficient for you, for My strength is made perfect in weakness" (2 Cor. 12:9). This echoes what I later read in Bloom: "Therefore, the first thought we ought to have when we do not tangibly perceive the divine presence, is a thought of *gratitude*" (emphasis mine).[45]

I read over the entire third prayer to the Theotokos again. It exuberantly lists all the good things that are the work of the Spirit and their ultimate goal: to glorify and praise Christ Jesus, in all things.

Beyond that, nothing really matters.

※

I KEEP WALKING BENEATH THE trees on this November morning, asking for help, and I think about the third prayer to the Theotokos and all I have read. I look up again into the branches I pass beneath. The afghan pines will retain their needles, but in a few weeks' time, almost all else will be completely bare here. As the cold deepens, soundless signals will begin deep in the trees. The rest of their chlorophyll will break down, and the green will disappear. Nutrients will be shuttled deep into the trees' roots, and when all is stored away and retreated inward, the trees will release the rest of their leaves in a final explosion of red and gold, a necessary abscission in a season that can't be prevented or slowed. Over the winter, they will rest.

This deliberate cutting away is essential. When the leaves fall, what really lies beneath is revealed.

My search for Mary, I realize, has been very much like this.

I've discovered through this season of failing and faltering prayer, of purposeless worry and fear, that God is and always has been in the in-between. I stop and look at the branches again. The light penetrates new spaces that were once covered in a thicket of greenness. Sky shines behind the wood in a pattern I've never seen before. Faith, I think, is like this. It's not just seeing things as they are on the surface: the painted face of Mary on an icon, the glance of sunrise off the checkered bark of a lacebark elm, or a child's flushed cheek. Faith is the experience of peering into the in-between and knowing truth exists when everything is covered in shadow. Faith is trusting what you cannot see and cannot discern on your own. Faith is asking for help because you can't do it all on your own and knowing with confidence that it will be delivered.

An elderly man, hunched over at his waist, approaches me with his exuberant puppy. She is checkered black and white, soft with that new-puppy fur, and all gangly legs and paws. When she sees me, she tugs frantically at her leash, dragging the man with her, desperate to climb me and lick my face. Her name is, perfectly, Happy.

"My wife and I wanted a puppy," the elderly man simply explains, his trembling and sun-spotted hands trying to corral her jumping and licking. I smile at him. They walk on, the elderly man shuffling a slow pace while Happy tumbles into the grass, sending leaves flying as she rolls.

I step off the path and walk on, too, into the field where a line of white aspens borders the water. I look up. Their unfallen leaves flash silver and gray in the wind and sound like the faintest choir of angels, clapping softly.

Urging me on.

❋ EIGHT ❋

Friends

I will also meditate on all Your work,
And talk of your deeds.
—PSALM 77:12

It is early morning on a Saturday in December, just a few weeks from the end of the Nativity Fast. The moon, three-quarters pregnant with light, swells in the predawn sky. I am driving today the 120 miles to Amarillo to see my writing critique group for our annual Christmas brunch, and I pull my car into the gas station to fuel up for the two-hour drive just as the brightest stars wink out. December weather is tediously unpredictable in its moods, and one never knows if the day will herald with bitterly cold winds, still and crisp air, or uncharacteristic warmth. This morning brings the first, and I pull my coat around myself as I step out of my car, the sky just beginning to glow in the east.

My writing critique group consists of a quartet of women of very different ages, walks of life, and beliefs. No two of us were born in the same decade or have lived similar lives. Suzi is the oldest of our quartet, a sprightly, spunky woman full

Friends

of wisdom, perception, and mischief. She's in her seventies and writing her powerful memoir. Donna, who is incredibly thoughtful, generous, and compassionate, is the next oldest. She has struck out with inspiring bravery to finally write the science fiction novel that she began in her twenties. And then there is Kim, our dear Kim: the effervescent, insightful, and kind woman who writes everything from biblical historical fiction to noir detective stories.

Although we all have lived wildly different lives, each of us was born with a calling that pulled us inexplicably together two years ago: the bone-deep desire to write. We call ourselves the Lone Star Women of Letters, and our friendship has been the shining, guiding light in some of my darkest days. Writing is a vulnerable process, and through it, we've revealed the innermost workings of our hearts. These women have come to know me and accept me like no one else, and their encouragement and love feed my soul.

I live the farthest away, but I don't mind the drive to see them every few months. The time I spend crossing into the Texas Panhandle from the Southern Plains is good time to think, question, and pray. As I merge my car north onto the asphalt interstate leading out of town, the sky warms with color even more, illuminating low cumulus clouds that have gathered these past mornings on the horizon.

It is a marvelous season of sunrises, these December mornings, for the sun cuts like a gold knife across the pale-yellow prairie grass, brittle and bent in winter, and slices everything into shades of gray and wheat. Along the western edges of the highway, black cotton fields are speckled with tufts of white. Most of the cotton has been stripped this time of year, but a few fields look as if they are dotted with snow. It only adds to the hush of soft colors this morning, these muted tones of winter that seep like water into every corner of sight.

As I drive, huge flocks of Canada geese lift from roadside fields and glassy playas in undulating sheets of black and gray and take flight. They catch my breath, those beautiful travelers moving as one living organism. Even from inside my car speeding along the highway, I hear their honks, joyfully demanding community on this solo morning. *Hurry, hurry,* they seem to say to each other. *The light is here.* A portion of sunrise catapults between the clouds and makes them glow like embers. *It's time to go.*

How do they know, I wonder, when it's time to lift together and fly? Does one goose move just right, angling toward inevitable flight, and the rest—those soulful, perceptive creatures—follow? Or is some undecipherable element of time-telling knit within them that activates with the light? I think of Met. Anthony's lovely analogy of imagining each new day as a "vast expanse of unsoiled snow" discovered in morning, untrodden and full of possibility.[46] The geese herald this morning in the same way for me with their focused flight. A gaggle departs and aligns into a V high above me, and we speed in opposite directions toward our different destinations.

IT IS STRANGE THAT I have driven this road so many times in my life that I know every curve and small-town overpass, yet every time I drive it, it always feels new, even on this morning. No other day of my life has the light been like the light of this day, nor these exact birds my co-travelers, nor the slowly moving clouds overhead casting shadows like these onto the land. This day, I know, will end, and no other day to follow will ever be exactly like it. The temporal tenuousness of it spellbinds me, and I feel the ache of it so badly I want the light and the colors and the birds of this moment to freeze that I might hang onto them for a little longer.

But it is not to be, I know. And at the heart of this temporary ache is a deep-seated truth I have always struggled with: that all things change and pass. Somewhere along the way—in constant childhood moves, maybe, or in bitter losses accompanying adulthood—I began to fear that truth, for so much of life felt dangerous and unpredictable, and therefore, unreliable. My earliest memories are laced with powerful, confusing losses: peering over the hospital bed of my grandmother hooked up to machines, the wild look of illness in my mother's eyes, the silent stretcher carrying a body to an ambulance while I waited alone in a car.

Many good things are suspended in memory, too, but it's the dissolve into uncertainty that seemed to heighten those feelings. I became very adept at anticipating the end before it actually came, so as not to be caught unprepared, and I learned to travel to the worst loss I could imagine in my heart before the loss even—or ever—happened.

"You're tenderhearted," I remember my grandpa saying to me once. His eyes shone with a bit of wonder with the statement, as if he might be proud of this trait in his family. I always took it as a compliment, but being tenderhearted means I feel things strongly.

Perhaps too strongly.

Now, when I begin to lean too far toward the edge of anticipatory grief, I catch myself in that mindset and work to shake it off. This moment is not to last, I know, but it is beautiful and God-given. I am reminded this day calls to me in *participatory beauty*, and God calls me to savor it, so I pull over at a rusting gas station halfway through my trip to write down these words and to pray a little. The Eternal has been and always will be, I remind myself. Nothing is lost. I know the things of myself that are earnest and honest and struggling to make sense of what's happening to me on this journey are all completely within God's sight and in His providence. This gives me comfort. I drive on, pondering these things.

And the word *ponder* gives me pause, for it is a word often used of Mary.

※

OF ALL THE GOSPEL AUTHORS, I feel St. Luke, the physician, writes with the most intimate and psychological eye of human experience. In his Gospel, he writes that he decided *"having had perfect understanding of all things from the very first*, to write to you an orderly account . . . that you may know the certainty of those things in which you were instructed" (Luke 1:3–4, emphasis mine). Saint Luke's Gospel reads to me, at times, like a biographical profile, for he includes details of ordinary human experience that could only have come from interviewing the people who encountered Christ. He not only peers into experiences of what happened, but references inner landscapes, too. For lack of a better word, St. Luke makes people feel *real* and makes their inner lives just as important as what happened to them or what they did.

You could say that St. Luke writes like someone who knows his subject matter intimately—a friend even. He does this especially with Mary. No other Gospel author references Mary's inner perspective the way St. Luke does, and his account of Christ's birth has always struck me, for he includes details about what Mary was thinking and feeling. In this passage, for example:

> *Now there were in the same country shepherds living out the fields, keeping watch over their flock by night. And behold, an angel of the Lord stood before them, and the glory of the Lord shone around them, and they were greatly afraid. Then the angel said to them, "Do not be afraid, for behold, I bring you good tidings of great joy which will be to all people. For there is born to you this day in the city of David a Savior, who is Christ the Lord. And this will be the sign to you: You will find a Babe wrapped in swaddling cloths, lying in a manger." And suddenly there was with the angel a multitude of the heavenly host praising God and saying: "Glory to God in the highest, And on earth peace, goodwill toward men!" So it was, when the angels had gone away from them into heaven, that the shepherds said to one another, "Let us now go to Bethlehem and see this thing that has come to pass, which the Lord has made known to us." And they came with haste and found Mary and Joseph, and the Babe lying in the manger. When they had seen Him, they made widely known the saying which was told them concerning this Child. And all those who heard it marveled at those things which were told them by the shepherds. But Mary kept all these things and pondered them in her heart. (Luke 2:8–19)*

The interior jumps out at me: Mary treasured all these words and *pondered* them in her heart. With what tenderness and respect St. Luke honors the Mother of God by including these precious details in his Gospel. I like to imagine him visiting with her in a lamplit room years after these events took place, asking her to recount, one more time, what happened the night the Savior Himself was born. Did her face change and soften at his question? Did her gaze pass through him and stop somewhere in her mind's eye on the cave where she gave birth? Did she surprise St. Luke by not just telling him facts, but also the innermost workings of her heart: how mysterious and beautiful she found the words conveyed by the shepherds. How she carried this strange miracle with her always. How she contemplated it with the same reverence she had felt when, nine months earlier, she'd pondered a different revelation from the archangel Gabriel (Luke 1:26–38).

As Mary finished her story, did her gaze return to St. Luke and the modest room in which they sat, now completely transformed by Christ's redemption of the world in which they lived? I like to imagine them looking at each other then: these two people who had long been friends and witnessed the greatest act of love in the history of the world. I like to imagine them nodding and smiling in silent acknowledgment of what they knew was the Truth, and what joy the rest of the world would come to know, as well.

My vision is complete conjecture, of course, but St. Luke's words are not. I can relate to pondering things deeply. It helps me not feel so alone, knowing that the Mother of God wondered, too, about all these things. And just like Mary, I have good friends who know the inner workings of my heart, too, and who never cease asking me to tell them my story.

※

OUR CHRISTMAS BRUNCH IS A great party, as always. On this special day, which I only get to celebrate once a year with these friends of mine, we feast on pastries and spreads, homemade quiches and sandwiches, and bright fruit shining like Christmas lights. After we eat, we exchange gifts: all the things a group of writers could imagine giving to each other. There are special writing sets, books, and pens. We give each other bookmarks, notes of encouragement, ornaments to document the year, and hilarious socks to keep feet warm while sitting at our desks pounding away at the keyboard. Most of all, there is laughter. Surrounded by the warm tones of Kim's home, we bask with full bellies and hearts in the simple joy of just being together: four women, miles and decades apart, gazing past the year we've had and into the future we hope for.

Telling the story of our stories, once again, to eager ears that never tire of listening.

My journey to know and understand Mary better illuminates this all, for she's been with these friends of mine, too. As they have read my words and helped me with each passage and season, Mary has become a part of their lives, too. "Sweet Brandi, I draw strength from your beautiful words as I sit alone in my car this cold and foggy morning," writes Suzi to me one day. It is a hard day for her. "But your writing has filled me with courage, and as I leave my car, I'm determined to make this day a blessed one."

It is all I ask for: that something from this year seeking out Mary, and the personal revelations I share, and everything I've learned might help someone else. Perhaps St. Luke shared that goal with Mary, too, and this is why she told him everything that was on her heart.

So that you may know the truth.

❈ NINE ❈

Miracles

Because she believed in a perfect way, she established at this instant, in this village wedding, the Kingdom of God.
—METROPOLITAN ANTHONY OF SOUROZH[47]

It is the Forefeast of the Nativity of Christ—Christmas Eve—and the air is heavy with anticipation. Members from our small congregation have gathered in our church on this bright and windy winter morning for the long prayer services of Orthros and the Royal Hours before the Vesperal Divine Liturgy of St. Basil the Great. Through the velvety, rose-scented air, the icons reflect golden candlelight and the passing flash of red vestments as our priest leads the services. Soon, all the red draping from the tables will be changed to gold to herald the newborn Savior of the world. We will go home, sleep, and rise again, God willing, to return here tomorrow morning. Then our celebration will, at last, arrive: salvation given in a Babe through a miraculous virgin birth. God has bent the heavens and the very order of nature itself to meet us here on earth.

There are not many in our small church this morning,

but those who have come have been waiting for this day for a long time: not just through the forty days of the Nativity Fast, but for most of our lives, it seems. Most of us here are converts, and Orthodox worship, we've learned, provides direct access to the Apostolic Church and a true experience of eternal worship. Coming to this place willingly as an adult after many years of searching leaves some of us converts breathless and a bit anxious, for having never had a Christianity or a Christmas worship like this, we don't want to lose it.

It is a miracle our small parish exists on the West Texas plains, and even more a miracle that now and then a stranger walks through the door to seek, question, or just satisfy their curiosity about what our small white building near a busy intersection and grocery store has to offer. When our front door creaks open and someone steps in, the angel's declaration echoes in my head: "I bring you good tidings of great joy which will be to all people" (Luke 2:10).

I AM THINKING A LOT about miracles during this season. My husband's grandfather, a kind, sweet man with whom I love to talk and whom I have gotten to know more in the last few years, collapsed unconscious in his home in early December. Rushed to the hospital, he remained unresponsive and on a ventilator, his brain activity indiscernible. There was no hope, the doctors implied, and so plans were made to honor the strict wishes he dictated in his do-not-resuscitate order.

My own grandparents are gone, and so my bond with Grandpa Schreiber is important. Last Christmas, we talked for two hours about his time growing up in upstate New York, the old stone Huguenot cottage he grew up in, and all the traveling he'd done in his life. I love seeing him when we get to visit my in-laws, for his face lights up in a huge smile when I walk through the door. It is painful to experience his sudden illness during the Christmas season, to grieve during a time that is supposed to be filled with so much joy.

I prayed to God for his care and to Mary to intercede for him. "Please take care of him," I asked her, but the possibility of healing seemed remote. In my heart of hearts, I wasn't sure much would change. How does one recover from indiscernible brain activity?

But on the Monday the doctors planned to turn his life support machines off, he woke up.

"How long was I out?" he asked my father-in-law when he could speak again.

When we got this news, I thought about Christ raising His beloved Lazarus from the dead. Christ, who is fully God, already *knew* what the outcome would be. He delayed answering the call to be by Lazarus's bedside in order to ensure that Lazarus had died and that there would be no question about the state of his body when He raised him. Despite knowing this miracle would occur and joy would return, Christ—who is also fully human—mourned the human condition and felt the bitterness of death and shared grief that separated Him from His beloved friend: "Therefore, when Jesus saw [Mary, the sister of Martha and Lazarus] weeping, and the Jews who came with her weeping, He groaned in the spirit and was troubled. . . . Jesus wept" (John 11:33, 35).

We wept, too, when we heard Grandpa Schreiber had woken up.

Miracles

I HAVE JUST FINISHED READING Fr. George Papadeas's book, *Why Did She Cry: The Story of the Weeping Madonna*, a firsthand account of the three miraculous weeping Madonnas that manifested to parishioners of St. Paul's Greek Orthodox Cathedral in the spring of 1960. Fr. Papadeas witnessed these miraculous images—all of which were paper-and-cardboard lithographs, including both Western and Eastern icons of the Virgin Mary—weep. Reading about the effects the icons had on thousands of Christian and non-Christian pilgrims sends chills down my spine. In my research about Mary, I have stumbled across many other references to miracle-performing icons and sites, from icons housed on Mount Athos to Lourdes to the Hill of Tepeyac where the Virgin of Guadalupe first revealed herself to Juan Diego. However, the weeping Madonnas of St. Paul's Cathedral feel closer to home, although the "divine signs" occurred sixty years ago in Long Island, far from my West Texas home.

Most interesting to me is that all three icons began crying in parishioners' homes. The world outside our churches is where we must spend most of our lives living out our faith. Kitchen corners, cramped offices, our car interiors on commutes, and weekend backyards are where we mostly live as Christians. I think about what faith and power must have been present in the apartment rooms of those families in the 1960s where these icons first began weeping: one small, inconspicuous tear at a time becoming streams that damaged their cardboard borders. What faith must have existed in the mundane setting of home that brought forth those tears, and what faith spread and kept them flowing! It is astonishing to me that over eight thousand pilgrims came to St. Paul's Cathedral to witness the tears of the Virgin Mary and to venerate those icons.[48] So many people. What an overwhelming testament to such faith.

When I return home from church on the Eve of the Nativity, I examine my favorite icon of the Theotokos, a version of the *Panagia Glykophilousa*, or "Sweet Kissing" icon, in which the Christ Child is cheek-to-cheek with His Mother, looking at her with affection. In this icon, He tenderly reaches up and touches her chin. The icon was a gift to my husband and me when our marriage was blessed, and it is filled with such gentleness and emotion that it lights something in my chest every time I look at it.

In the flickering candlelight of our home icon corner, I examine Mary's hands and fingers where they hold her Son. She holds Him tentatively, as she always does, turning Him slightly to present Him to the world. One small foot of the Christ Child arches upward as He leans into His Mother's embrace, another beautiful detail I love. This darkened corner of my home, where this icon rests, has heard many prayers and been witness to many joys and sorrows. I wonder, in the waning light of the day, what I would do if I saw a tear pool in the corner of Mary's eye?

Would I even believe it?

Would I need to?

※

MARY IS AND ALWAYS HAS been associated with miracles. She was an integral part of Jesus' first miracle, which propelled the beginning of His ministry on Earth.

Jesus could have done a great many things to reveal His power to the world for the first time. He could have stood on top of the temple and performed a miracle for the masses below. He could have gone immediately to the high priests, prelates, and Roman authorities and awed them with His power. However, of all the places He could have chosen to begin His transformative work, and of all the people He could have picked to be present with Him at this pivotal moment, He chose a poor village wedding at Cana in Galilee, which He attended with His Mother and disciples (John 2:1–2).

Metropolitan Anthony, in his marvelous book *God and Man*, sets the scene perfectly: "Long before hearts have been seized with joy," he writes, "long before they are overflowing with that life, the human conditions for joy begin to run out. No doubt the lights are going dim, the bread has been eaten and the wine is failing."[49] This simple, humble wedding in a region that is mostly Gentile is filled with the most ordinary of human life. Indeed, the "human conditions for joy" have long been running out, and it's time for the Messiah to reveal Himself—almost. But first Mary, a keen observer, notices the wine has run out.

I like to imagine this scene, too: a room in a humble house lit with lamps, a table with food and cups set out for drinking. Across the space, perhaps in seats of honor or standing near a doorway, the bride and groom smile and meet the guests who have traveled so far to be here, including Mary, Christ, and His disciples. Orthodox tradition teaches that Mary being there indicates she may have been a relative of the bride or groom, so there is a strong sense of familial bond: joy, pride, and a swelling of heart for seeing the beloveds married and all the families and friends celebrating with them.

But there is a humbleness here, too, that is touching, for the love Mary had for this family is evident in her concern for their failing resources. "She felt for the family," writes Fr. David Smith, "who couldn't afford to celebrate their children's wedding properly. . . . Without wine, the celebration would end very quickly, and everyone would go home."[50] She knows the family deserves to celebrate more, but they cannot. The primary resource for joy is depleted.

So Mary says something to her Son that is so simple its impact and context are often overlooked. She says to Him, "They have no wine" (John 2:3).

It is such an ordinary statement Mary makes to her Son, but the moment is full of power. Mary sees the empty wine cups and the guests' restlessness that soon will lead to their exit, and she understands the loss of joy that will ensue if, at such a time, the family cannot continue their celebration. She is in this moment exactly the way we know her to be through millennia of writings, encounters, and miracles: caring, benevolent, and concerned about the workings of our ordinary lives. But more than that, she embodies what Met. Anthony describes as "intercessory prayer defined as a presence."[51]

Mary knows her Son. She knows who He is, and "she makes the act of being there, fully and completely involved" in the presence of God by getting His attention in the midst of the guests. She meets His eyes and tells Him her concerns. She asks Christ, without asking a question at all, to reveal Himself, to give to the wedding party and its guests "what the earth is now refusing, the gift . . . that is at the same time of the order of eternal life."[52] She asks this not because she expects she can command it as His Mother, but because she believes fully in who He is. She knows He can perform a miracle.

And Christ asks her a question in turn: "Woman, what does your concern have to do with Me? My hour has not yet come" (John 2:4). To the modern ear, this sounds harsh and dismissive, but "woman" was "a title of respect and distinction" in ancient Jewish society.[53] Christ is asking His Mother, whom He respects deeply, to confirm, out loud, what she's asking of Him and why this matters now since His time for public disclosure has not arrived. "My hour has not yet come," continues Met. Anthony, "is a statement that pertains to eternal life and the coming of the Kingdom, and not simply to the magistery of a miracle-worker."[54] In other words, He asks Mary why the wine running out matters *now*, not because He doesn't care about the marriage feast, but because Mary's statement of faith is one of the first in the entire Gospel.

Christ is listening for her response.

And Mary responds as a believer.

She doesn't admonish Him for questioning what a mother wants or answer His question with another question. Instead, she answers him with *action*. She turns to the servants and tells them, "Whatever He says to you, do it" (John 2:5). Her statement to others is a first testament of belief in who He is, "a total, integral, unlimited act of faith, the faith on which the Annunciation was founded; the faith that she bore witness to in being the mother of the Child-God."[55]

And Christ, with His Mother, a first, true believer, beside Him, knows then His time *has* come and changes "the exhausted waters, the useless waters, the waters soiled by washing" into brimming vats of beautiful, red, flowing wine. It is "the wine of the Kingdom . . . a revelation of something greater."[56]

The servants, bewildered and astonished, I imagine, draw this new wine from the washing vats and respond with action as well. They take it, as Christ commands them, to the master of the feast, who exclaims, "You have kept the good wine until now!" (John 2:8–10). The marriage celebration can continue, but more than that, the first sign—a miracle—has occurred. Great and present belief allowed God to reveal Himself by changing the very order of nature. Christ listened to His Mother, and He responded.

The unveiling of the Kingdom of God could not have happened any other way, with any other person than the Theotokos. It wasn't Christ's disciples, forever missing the mark, who noticed the failing wine, knew what Christ could do, and pressed God to reveal Himself in the simple company of a poor village wedding and its servants. The disciples didn't get it yet. In fact, His disciples "believed in Him" *after* they witnessed the miracle (John 2:11). It was the Theotokos, Christ's very Mother, who had been witness to all these things from the very beginning, and it was the Theotokos to whom Christ listened and responded.

It makes perfect sense, then, that she is forever associated with miracles, not because she is the miracle-maker or the miracle-forcer, but because she listens and observes, and in turn, asks her Son to intercede for those she cares about. The glory belongs to God, but the act of faith that helped prompt "the good wine" was hers. Her power as a key intercessor for all Christians has been evident in this way from the very beginning of the Gospel. "One human person was present to God," Met. Anthony reminds me.[57]

Just one person who believed. That is all it took.

My mind drifts back to the wooden cross covered in

milagros, tiny miracles, that the shopkeeper gave me. I keep it next to my bed to remember her in my prayers. Lately, I have been holding it against my heart and my belly, the cold tin of the tiny charms pressing through my clothes. I don't pray for a miracle; I just ask to believe that anything is possible.

※

I STAND ON MY BACK porch early this morning, two days after the Feast of the Nativity. The gray aftershocks of the first rain we've had all month hang in the air: slate-colored sky, black limbs, a breeze so light the wind chimes strike only one slow, mournful note at a time that rings forever in the fog. *Ding... Ding... Ding.* Not even the geese quake above me this morning, and the only other sounds are the dense raindrops on the wet leaf piles. It is so achingly peaceful it rends my heart in two.

Not long after Grandfather Schreiber awoke, he suddenly began to decline again. Unable to be transported home or to a specialized nursing facility, he was placed on hospice in the hospital, and fell asleep, as we Orthodox describe death, very early this morning.

For a brief moment, my prayers *had* been answered. I believe that firmly. I asked Mary to care for him, to give him comfort, and to ease grieving hearts, and I asked God for healing. And it happened. We lived, however momentarily, in the inexplicable joy of *what seemed impossible*—hope transformed for us like the washing water because a beloved man, unconscious, unresponsive, and unable to breathe on his own, suddenly woke up and rejoined us on the very day his life was supposed to end. But it wasn't meant to last, just like the physical wedding wine wasn't meant to flow forever. It was meant to be drunk.

It was meant to be celebrated.

The miracle we'd experienced was when we could look at each other and say, "God is in this place." The miracle was the unexpected joy, the extra conversation, the time our busy and distracted minds whipped back in God's direction before the delayed death arrived. It happened, and we could talk about it and wonder, as so many times Mary did, what it meant.

"When we speak of miracles," Fr. Papadeas writes,

> We somehow think automatically in terms of the healing from some physical ailment. That is, for a paralytic to walk, a blind person to see, a deaf person to hear . . . [we] should never lose sight of the healing of the soul, which is a major miracle. These miracles of soul-healings go unheralded for the most part, simply because of their relatively subjective and private matter.[58]

The healing of the soul *is* a major miracle. I think about how much my own perspectives on my faith have changed over these past months, about the effect searching for Mary has had on my bigger understanding of God's grace, action, and love in my life. It is miracle enough that I am here on this journey, searching out these things, trying to understand what I can't quite fully perceive and might never fully grasp. And it is true: a great portion of my soul has been healed in this process.

But I'm going to miss my Grandpa Schreiber terribly.

I choke back a sob and look up just as a flock of black grackles soars soundlessly above the trees. They flap their wings in unison and ride on the updraft of their work, their beaks pointed skyward.

Yes, there is always room for the miraculous, even in a season of grief.

I am pregnant.

Christ is born. Glorify Him.

❃ TEN ❃

Wives

> *Now in the sixth month the angel Gabriel was sent by God to a city of Galilee named Nazareth, to a virgin betrothed to a man whose name was Joseph, of the house of David. The virgin's name was Mary.*
> —LUKE 1:26—27

It is February now, and the morning is cloaked in cold, low-lying fog. As I move across my back porch, I feel the crystalline moisture bump against my cheeks. It is like moving through a frozen cloud, thick as cotton. However, it isn't the silvery, dense air that surprises me this morning. It is the absolute silence I meet. No Canada geese honk and pulse above me in purposeful movement today. They are all gone.

They leave as suddenly as they arrive, these migratory birds, somehow deciding one morning to lift from the area waters and fields and not return. After months of hearing their boisterous cries, the buzz of their wings with the breaking of the dawn, and their cacophony at the playa, I walk to where they should be flapping at the water's edge and find they aren't there. Only the mallards and a few local white geese remain. Their soft honking suddenly seems small compared to all the noise that was once here. The remaining birds float and preen their feathers, bobbing among discarded down and other feathered detritus, the only things the Canada geese have left behind.

It always breaks my heart a little to see the waters and fields so empty each February, to hear the air so suddenly quiet and still. The geese won't return for another nine months, and during that time, I miss them. I reach down and untangle a long gray feather from the grass, a souvenir of the geese's overwintering on these stark plains, and walk down to the water's edge. A plain brown mama mallard tracks me with her soft eyes.

"It's just us now," I say, my words unexpectedly loud in all this quiet. She steps into the water and pushes off, the movement barely making a sound. From far above, I imagine she is indiscernible from the gray and white water she drifts in. But then again, for most of the winter she's had to live on the edge of thousands of visiting geese, sharing the playa's resources and dodging their large, confident bodies. Now the water is all hers again. I look out across the wide expanse of empty water to where tall grasses grow at the northern edge of the playa. If this little hen is paired with a drake already, she'll build a small nest of sticks and feathers somewhere in those grasses and have her own little brood by the end of spring.

I touch my belly where my own miracle grows, the feeling of Mary so suddenly present. The emptiness and silence here fill with possibility and peace. We have the whole spring and summer, this little female duck and I, to wait together for what will come.

Before I walk on, I notice a male mallard drifting close by. Her drake, perhaps. His head shines with iridescent green cast in black, like a beetle's shell. He will stay with her until the mating season ends and her ducklings come, but then he'll move on and leave the duckling caretaking to the mama. Hardly a courtship, betrothal, and marriage by human standards, but a divine and necessary design that presses life forward on these waters. The February chill whips around me, a reminder spring is still far off, but the ducks seem unaffected, their deep layers of down keeping them warm in the water.

I head across the bare fields back toward home, to my waiting husband, and the ducks' soft quacking fades behind me.

❦

BETROTHAL. THIS TERM HAS A completely different meaning than our modern *engagement*. Whereas today an engagement can be broken off before a wedding for any number of personal reasons that are entirely up to the couple, betrothal in the ancient world meant an agreement or contract made between parties or families that had just as much weight and consequence as if the couple were actually married. Betrothals (and ultimately marriage) were, in fact, quite often arranged through negotiations of families, something that wasn't taken lightly. The promise of marriage was just as binding as the marriage itself.

According to the *Jewish Encyclopedia*, the act of betrothal was "to contract an actual though incomplete marriage . . . when the agreement had been entered into, it was definite and binding upon both groom and bride, who were considered as man and wife in all legal and religious aspects, except that of actual cohabitation." In fact, betrothals were so significant, they could "only be dissolved by a formal divorce."[59]

I think about my own betrothal story, what feels like so many years ago. Inside a dusty phone booth one hot summer in Spain where I was studying for two weeks, I heard my now-husband's voice, tinged with emotion, cross the ocean: "I think we should get married." At the time, we lived in different states because we were both in graduate school. We were two young twenty-somethings in love, trying to figure out our next steps on our own as best we could in a world that felt huge with possibility. My heart jumped at his words, arrived at with his characteristic thoughtfulness and logic. My husband is not one to rush into decisions, and I knew a suggestion of marriage must have been something he had thought deeply and carefully about for a while. "Let's not wait," he said.

"Okay," I returned slowly, leaning against the glass door of the phone booth, letting the warmth of his statement sink in. I had been planning to apply for jobs in the state in which he lived and get established somewhere close so we could keep dating. We knew our relationship was destined for marriage, but I didn't know he wanted to marry me *now*. His suggestion filled me with joy.

"Okay," I said again, this time more enthusiastically. "Let's get married!" And that was it! There were no negotiations between our families, as in the ancient world, and no contract or dowry that had to be agreed upon. The only plans that mattered were the ones we were making for our own lives. We trusted each other with this promise and vowed to see it through. And we did. A few months later, I had a ring, and within the year, we were married.

That was almost thirteen years ago.

But what about Mary's betrothal to Joseph? What can Mary teach me about my own marriage and role as a wife today? I pick up *The Life of the Virgin Mary, the Theotokos*, an incredible tome on the complete life of the Virgin Mary compiled by Holy Apostles Convent, and read. The first thing that becomes clear is that Orthodox teaching and tradition are quite explicit on the importance and purpose of Mary's betrothal to Joseph. Their story begins long before they ever met with her vow of chastity.

According to the Protoevangelium of James, an important popular, apocryphal text on the life of Mary written around AD 150, Mary was dedicated to the temple by her parents when she was three years of age.[60] Growing up in the temple, she devoted herself to prayer, the study of Scripture, and the contemplation of God, as well as to weaving, a skill she was apparently quite good at: "Apocryphal sources record that she was constant in prayer and her appearance was beautiful and glorious; hardly any one could look into her face. She occupied herself with wool-work, so that even in her tender years she achieved such skill as to surpass old women."[61] Multiple church fathers, including Saints Ambrose, Ephraim the Syrian, John of Damascus, and Gregory Palamas write about the time Mary spent in the temple and the development of her virtues as a result of her intense focus on God. Saint Gregory Palamas, in particular, likened Mary to "the model of the hesychastic life" and "the first to take it upon herself to pray unceasingly":

> According to St. Gregory, her asceticism therein did not lead her to come to an understanding of the grace received from the time of her

conception, but to learn more of the nature of the sins of Adam. . . . She would pray for the human race and God's great mercy. She understood the most excellent way to converse with God was through holy silence and silence of the mind. Hence, she withdrew from the world and put away all earthly things. Through this, by God's grace, she ascended to contemplation of Him.[62]

Mary learned at a very young age to focus on holiness, and as a result, "being God-inspired, dedicated her virginity to the Lord."[63] Saint John of Damascus writes that "she became an abode of every virtue, turning her mind from every worldly and carnal desire. This was fitting for her who was to conceive God within herself. She kept her soul and body virginal, for He is Holy and finds rest among the holy. Therefore, she sought and strove after holiness and was shown to be holy and a wondrous temple for the most high God."[64]

Through her intense contemplation, prayer, and devotion, Mary became purity itself. It is difficult to grasp in today's highly individualized, sexually "revolutionized" world the importance of purity and remaining a virgin. For most of us, this concept has been lost. But a vow of purity was then, as now for some clergy, monks, and nuns, a vehicle that removed physical distraction and temptation and made space for more spiritual endeavors, the acquisition of virtues, and serving God through prayer, acts of charity, and contemplation.

Perhaps she might have remained in the temple serving the Lord her entire life, but when Mary was about thirteen years old, it was decided that since she had achieved maturity (i.e., womanhood), she had to leave the temple. At that time, Jewish custom required that females of age endeavor to be married, but according to tradition, Mary balked: "She assigned the following reasons for her resolve to remain a virgin: that both she and her parents had devoted her to the service of the Lord and that she herself had vowed to never lie with a man."[65] Mary had dedicated herself, mind and body, to purity for God. The idea of being forced into a traditional wedded life, including a relationship with a man and subsequent children, must have been agonizing.

I stop here and think about the incredible consequences this must have had for her. Tradition teaches that both of her parents had died about three years earlier when she was around ten years old, so as an only child, Mary was utterly and completely alone. The temple, where she had served and dedicated herself to the Lord for so many years, was her only home. Now the high priest demanded that she leave since she was of marriageable age. What could she do? Ancient Jerusalem was not a place in which an unmarried woman could make a living or survive on her own. The social order and law required females to marry, but Mary was headstrong in declining, an act unheard of at that time.

Afraid of forcing her to break her vow of chastity, which would have displeased God greatly, but knowing they had no other options for keeping a girl entering womanhood in the temple, the high priests then came up with a plan: to "try to ascertain to whom Mary should be entrusted."[66] If Mary couldn't stay in the temple, then she had to be betrothed to someone worthy who would care for her and honor her dedication and vow to God, as well as provide for her since she was a single Jewish female without living relatives of her own. The priests cast lots to see which tribe this task would fall to, and the tribe of Judah was chosen. Then—and this is interesting—"the priest announced that all eligible *widowers* of Judah be summoned."

Why widowers? Because the high priests were looking for someone to *entrust* Mary to, someone who could essentially be a guardian and protector and who would honor her vow of chastity while also providing her with safety and support in Jewish society. Joseph, who was chosen by a divine sign, fit that bill. Orthodox tradition teaches that he was a carpenter of about eighty years of age and had previously been married for about forty years. From his first marriage, he had seven children: James, Jude, Simon, Joses, Salome, Esther, and a third daughter whose name isn't consistently recorded.[67] By being betrothed to Mary, a mere thirteen-year-old girl, he could serve as an older guardian and protector, while also fulfilling the law and the expectations of the priests of the temple.

This, however, was a burdensome task, and tradition records that Joseph balked, too. An ancient icon in Kariye Djami (the modern Church of the Holy Savior) in Constantinople depicts Joseph escorting Mary to his house. It is a tense scene portraying an uncertain man. "This subject is rarely depicted," the authors write, "but it portrays Joseph striding forward and, curiously, and almost unsatisfactorily, [turning] around to catch a glimpse of Mary. The rapid pace of their movements is shown by the fluttering drapery around their feet."[68] Joseph is almost hurrying away from Mary, his perplexing newfound responsibility, and, perhaps, from the watchful eyes of the townsfolk. He was an old man, after all, and Mary was "younger than [his] grandsons."[69] The idea of being betrothed to such a young girl after so many years of previous marriage and a rich family life surely made him feel ridiculous. What was his purpose here, and why was this God's will?

He would soon learn, and so would Mary (Matt. 1:18). First, however:

> *According to Hebrew custom . . . the betrothal preceded the actual marriage by a period varying in length, but not exceeding twelvemonth in the case of a maiden. In the east, courtship with the prospective bride was unknown. At the betrothal, the bridegroom, personally or by deputy, handed the bride a piece of money or a letter, it being expressly stated in each case that the man thereby espoused the woman. At the time of their betrothal, Joseph and Mary were poor. Accordingly, their betrothal must have been the simplest, and the dowry settled as the smallest possible.*[70]

From that moment on, "Mary was the betrothed wife of Joseph. Their relationship was sacred . . . both parties were regarded and treated in law (as to inheritance, adultery, need of formal divorce), as if they had been actually married, except as regarded their physically consummating the marriage."[71]

Mary and Joseph had now made a promise. They'd entered into a contract, spiritual and temporal. Mary had to trust that Joseph would protect her, keep her safe, provide for her, and honor her vow. And Joseph, in turn, was bound to a young girl as if he were actually married to her, so that if anything happened to break that contract, she would be subject to the consequences of the law.

This is why Mary's betrothal to Joseph was so crucial, and why in Orthodox Christianity it's absolutely sacrilegious to believe they were a couple who had biological children together after the birth of Christ or that Joseph ever had a physical relationship with Mary at all. How could an old man—or any man for that matter—possibly imagine having a sexual relationship with the Mother of God, a teenager who had taken a vow of chastity to serve the Lord her entire life? Indeed, how could any man stomach consummating a marriage to the woman who had been entrusted to his care when he had witnessed the miracle of her birthing the Messiah? Mary maintained incredible trust and faith in her betrothal to Joseph. Had he been someone different with darker intentions or someone who broke his promise to God and the high priests, Mary's story might have been different.

It reminds me again how much I must trust God in my own marriage, which has been full of its own sweetness and bitterness, as all marriages are. I think about that young twenty-something I was and the decisions I was making about my future. My husband and I were guided by God because we loved each other, but we were also eager to figure it out on our own, relying on our own wisdom and tenacity, as most young engaged couples in love do. Over the years, that leaning "on [our] own understanding" (Prov. 3:5 NKJV) failed us, and many times this was the impetus for us to remember who is in charge.

Mary, on the other hand, had to entirely trust those around her who were making her marriage decisions for her. She also had to trust that God was ultimately in control of everything that was happening and would protect her. She had to have faith that she was supposed to leave the temple and the only security she'd ever known, enter into a marriage contract with an old man she'd never met before, and engage in an entirely new family life—one that might not be totally receptive to her. Imagine Joseph explaining to his grown children who she was, why she'd been entrusted to him, and that he was now betrothed to her. Although we don't have any sources that document his children's reactions, I can imagine what it must have been like to see their baffled expressions; they may perhaps have felt even a tinge of hostility at the news. Imagine their father, now an old widower, betrothed to this strange girl from the temple.

It makes the icon in Kariye Djami seem very accurate.

I can't imagine the fear or hesitancy that might have crept up in her at such a prospect. But Mary trusted God ceaselessly, and in that process had to learn to trust Joseph, too. That's incredibly humbling. I realize this reflects the rhythm of my own marriage, matured many years after standing in that hot, dusty phone booth. Marriage is a reliance on God's guidance and grace to teach me how to love, trust, and care for another person, especially when it's hard or painful. My husband and I made a promise to each other, and through some of the darkest times of our lives, we've endured—not because we eventually figured it all out, but because we had to admit our powerlessness before God. We had to trust and bow to His will.

I think about Mary and realize that being a wife means relying less on my own abilities and strength, which so often fail or disappoint, and relying more on God to guide my steps in my marriage. I need His help every day.

Mary, through her incredible example, reminds me to ask for it.

A FEW DAYS LATER THE cold lifts, and the quiet skies soon feel normal. The Canada geese are now hundreds of miles away, making their thousand-mile journeys back toward the north. I think about them and wonder where they've stopped to feed and rest. I pray for their safe travels and their babies, which they'll hatch at the farthest corners of our hemisphere.

The silence they leave behind begins to fill with other possibilities: spring, the hope of rain, roots that begin to awaken. I lie in bed one night with a gentle lamplight filling the room and feel my belly again. Already it is rounding, an unexplainable mystery taking shape inside. I am bursting with wonder, joy, and a little trepidation, the hopes of all I can't yet see filling my imagination. My husband lies beside me and puts a hand on my stomach, the feeling warm and soft. We can't yet feel the baby move, but we will soon.

We fall asleep to that tenderness, as quiet as a prayer, and drift on our own waters of dreams.

❈ ELEVEN ❈

Sorrows

> *We will fare far better if, like the Theotokos, we answer the call of the messenger, saying, "Behold the servant of the Lord. Let it be done according to your word."*
> —SCOTT CAIRNS[72]

On my walk this afternoon, I touch a bough of a Bradford pear. These trees line the sidewalk of the house next to mine, and I pass through their shade in summer, see the cracked sky between their spindly, bare branches in winter. From my office window, I watch them explode into clouds of white blossoms in March, a sure sign that spring is here. This afternoon, however, the bough I touch is still a gaunt gray, but all along its edges runs a new texture: tiny, bulbous fissures of fresh growth. Buds of leaves and blossoms, just beginning to crack open to heave through the gray. Hidden things coming into view out of a skeleton of black, not yet born.

Sorrows

WE HAD A BAD DOCTOR'S appointment last week. Early testing revealed there might be something wrong with the baby, a chance of a disorder.

I had been waiting for a phone call on blood screening results. It was quite common, I was told, for someone my age to have this type of screening done. The worn, laminated spiral with tables of "what if" fractions and percentages the genetic counselor had shown us at my first ultrasound seemed to confirm that maybe testing was a good idea. Although my husband and I had no histories of genetic disorders in our families, I was concerned enough about the "big" conditions to have my blood drawn. It would be fun, too, to know the baby's sex early on, as the blood test promised. We already had boy and girl names picked out. Which one would we get to use? We'd find out soon, the genetic counselor told us. I could soon buy baby clothes. Decide on which colors to drape the nursery. Choose a blue pallet of stars or a pink pallet of roses for the baby's crib.

At a routine checkup a week later, however, a talkative nurse let slip that the results were in, needed to be discussed, that there was "something, and we're so glad you came in today because this is why we like to talk to you in person instead of call." Panic immediately set in. I turned to look at my husband, who'd accompanied me to this appointment with the simple hopes of hearing the baby's heartbeat on a Doppler. His face was stricken, gone white. I turned back to the nurse, who immediately realized her mistake and tried to backtrack.

"Oh, don't worry. The doctor will explain it to you."

"But something is wrong? With the results? With the baby?"

"Well, I can't tell you yet, but we're really glad you came in today so the doctor can talk to you in person."

"So then something is wrong?"

"Well . . . I'll just let the doctor explain."

So something is wrong, I thought. I felt fear, cruelly gnarled, run like a rough rope down my spine, snagging all my nerve endings. My husband heaved forward, put his head into his hands. I started to tremble, said a prayer for help. We were in a small, hot examination room at the back of the clinic where the ventilation didn't reach. The doctor was running behind with other patients. Each time the nurse came in to check on us, she tried to repair the damage she'd done by hinting at the results. Each time we got more scared.

"Oh, you're really worried, aren't you?" she asked once. "Don't worry. *It's not that serious.*" But anything having to do with the baby was serious when couched in those terms. She looked at us and asked if we just wanted her to hand us the results. I froze. I was afraid if I read them, I wouldn't understand what they said. I wanted an expert, someone who could tell me *exactly* what was going on, to give me the information and give it to me fully. We declined, asked how much longer it would be until we could see my doctor. "Soon," the nurse said. "She's finishing up with a patient."

But *soon* meant getting moved to another room, waiting another half hour in agony for my doctor to see us.

The nurse entered again. "I'm just going to leave these results here on the table, in case you want to look at them," she said. She turned them upside down on the cabinet. Now the problem of telling us the truth wasn't hers anymore. It was ours, if we were brave enough to face what was on the paper. I felt manipulated but still too terrified to read the results. I grabbed my husband's hand so I wouldn't rush across the room to the papers left casually on the yellow laminate counter.

A few minutes later, the nurse entered one more time and noticed the papers were still untouched. She knew she had messed up. "I'm just going to give this to you now," she said nervously, shoving two sheets of paper at us and pointing to one of the results printed at the top. "Look!" she said. "You're going to have a little boy!"

A boy? I thought. *A little boy?* I couldn't process the statement. The gender reveal was completely overwhelmed by lists of tests run, probabilities, and other information printed in rows and percentages around his male gender symbol.

Him. A little boy.

A dancing little boy, I would see through my tears an hour later on an ultrasound. A swimming little boy in my womb, kicking his legs into the void. In the middle of his chest, just above the faint line of a developing diaphragm, a strong, pulsing heartbeat emerged in black-and-white textures. He moved in and out of our line of view as my doctor moved the ultrasound wand over my belly.

My little boy, just beginning to reveal his own secrets in the depths of darkness.

※

I HAVE NEVER FELT LOVE like this, this protective, tidal, bone-crushing love. What is so small, seemingly frail, and completely innocent pulses inside me, and I want nothing more in the world than for him to be okay. I pray for that day and night. The helplessness I feel about this situation blots out everything else.

I release the pear branch this afternoon and walk on with my husband down to the playa. We have been on a rollercoaster of ups and downs since my doctor's appointment. Periods of faith that everything will be okay are almost always followed by fear that it won't, that he'll be born with a condition that might make his life difficult. We could find out for sure with amniocentesis, but we decide against any further testing. I don't want to dread the months until another, potentially dangerous test reveals something that we may or may not find out in the future anyway. I want joy during this time, and I want my little one to feel that joy in my body, not my fear.

Yet, it's hard to be at this particular threshold of suffering. It makes everything else in life that felt difficult before pale in comparison. I am gutted by my husband's tears and angry at myself for even having the screening test done, for wondering if my little boy would fall into those bleak columns of negative statistics based on my age outlined in the genetic counselor's spiral. I am angry and ashamed I wanted to know too much. Although the screening test indicated almost nonexistent chances for Down syndrome and other major chromosomal disorders, including fatal ones, it gave us a wild card instead. A chance exists the test could be wrong, but I feel foolish, weak, and small. I feel I am drowning in all the uncertainty.

I think about Scott Cairns' *The End of Suffering: Finding Purpose in Pain*, a poignant and profound "study on suffering," and what sense he makes of pain and grief in light of being an Orthodox Christian. "Knowledge of 'our weakness' is the beginning of all that is good and beautiful," he writes, for "this knowledge . . . can . . . bear witness of the inexhaustible enormity of our God. It can give to us a comforting assurance that even if *we* are constrained by our limitations, our God and His reality continue to extend far beyond what we can make of them."[73] I try to embrace that smallness, that feeling of helplessness, and turn it over to a God who is the Maker of everything seen and unseen.

We walk to the trail circling the playa. A soft wind is blowing from the west, bringing in long swaths of clouds that tinge the sky gray and yellow. The air is warming, and although the grass is still golden, the lacebark elms and globe willow have already begun to bud. "Look," I say, pulling down a branch from a live oak. A tiny acorn is just beginning to bloom on the stem. These are exactly the little things I want to show my son someday. I clutch my husband's hand as we walk through a bare Eden, needing to feel God close by.

Mary, help us, I silently pray as we walk. *Intercede with your Son, through whom all things were made, including this little one. Make him whole. Make him well. Let him start out life strong. If there is a price to pay, take from me whatever is needed. Just don't give him this.* I know that God isn't exacting payment or punishment, but I offer it up anyway. I wish, then, to know the prayers that Mary must have prayed when she was pregnant with Jesus, in the midst of so much uncertainty. Her own role as an expectant mother, confused and awaiting the unknown with perfect trust in God, hits me in the chest. I feel all the joy of possibility and the wrenching sorrow of powerlessness over our children's suffering.

I understand now, I pray. *What it means to be filled with so much sorrow and love at the same time.*

In the Orthodox Church, Mary is considered the greatest of mourners as well as the greatest of intercessors. This is because, as the Mother of God and the human closest to Christ, she fully experienced all the sorrows and joys of her Lord, including His crucifixion. In fact, before Christ is crucified, He warns His disciples of the suffering and grief to come:

> *These things I have spoken to you, that you should not be made to stumble. They will put you out of the synagogues; yes, the time is coming that whoever kills you will think that he offers God service. And these things they will do to you because they have not known the Father nor Me. . . . I still have many things to say to you, but you cannot bear them now. . . . Most assuredly, I say to you that you will weep and lament, but the world will rejoice; and you will be sorrowful, but your sorrow will be turned into joy. (John 16:1–3, 12, 20)*

At His crucifixion, these disciples who were told about this coming suffering, sorrow, and subsequent joy scattered in fear, but it was Mary, the women, and St. John who stood nearby, faced the sorrow head-on, and watched Him die (John 19:25).

As the Mother of Jesus, however, Mary experienced the horror most intensely. She stood by helplessly as the Jewish and Roman authorities beat, stripped, and murdered her earthly Son, the Flesh of her flesh, but she also watched them murder God Himself. What agony it must have been to have carried Him, given birth to Him, raised Him, watched His miracles, experienced His power, absorbed His love, witnessed the healing and redemption He brought to the world He so loved—only to watch Him die a violent, cruel criminal's death at its hands. The prophecy Simeon shared with her was more than fulfilled: a sword pierced her own soul, also (Luke 2:35).

What other human being could feel that love and sorrow more powerfully than the Mother who bore Him? And who else could understand such suffering? The God of the entire world—its Maker and Lover, its Healer and Protector—was killed by the very people He came to redeem, and Mary had to see the mangled and bloody body of her Son as a result. Orthodox iconography of the taking down from the Cross frequently features Mary, in her sorrow holding the lifeless body of her Son. She is pictured weeping, bent toward Him or holding Him from behind, and tenderly touching her face to His—a reversal of all the tenderness in the icons of the Christ Child in her embrace.

Such grief makes Mary a special intercessor because she can relate to humanity in a way no other human can. She knows what it means to feel the ultimate loss of a child. *The Lamentations of the Theotokos*, written in the ninth century by St. Symeon and sung during Matins on Holy Saturday, are a series of painful cries the Theotokos utters about her Son's crucifixion and burial:

> *Alas! Son older than the Mother! What burial lamentations and what funeral hymns should I sing? . . . Then I was freed from the pains of birth, but now at Thy funeral I accept all grief! Many times I remained sleepless, holding Thee as an infant to my breast, but now Thou dost sleep among the dead.*[74]

How hard it must have been in that moment to remember that her grief would soon turn into joy, also.

At the entrance of our church, an icon of *Mary, Joy of All Who Sorrow* hangs on the wall. Framed in gold and rusty red—a hue reminiscent of dried blood—it features the Theotokos standing in front of large, blooming flowers of Paradise. All around her, flanking her on both sides, are rows of people asking for her intercession: the sick, the lame, the dying, the suffering. Mary looms above them all, her figure dwarfing them. She stands with her arms outstretched and looks to be listening to them intently, her face and head angled down to catch their prayers.

It is a depiction of her power as intercessor, as someone who is sensitive to the suffering of the entire world. She stands both in Paradise, with the sun and the moon in corners just above her, but also on Earth, surrounded by the people who pray to her. Angels assist in her work, ministering and tending to the people around her.

The original icon of this type was authenticated as miraculous in 1688 when a woman was healed of her disease after hearing a voice telling her to find the icon and celebrate it with her priest. Another version of the icon was authenticated in 1888 when a chapel housing it was struck by lightning and the icon, miraculously, survived, albeit with coins forever fused to its frame. Both icons are associated with healing and miracles.

I pay special attention to this icon now when I walk into church. I count my family and my unborn baby among the ranks of those anxiously petitioning Mary for help. I can see us all folded into the throngs of the faithful, needing help, needing healing, looking up to her outstretched hands and being ministered to, invisibly, by angels.

Sorrows

AFTER OUR DOCTOR'S APPOINTMENT, I carefully cut one precious black-and-white ultrasound photo from the strip of four and place it on top of our icon of Mary in our icon corner. *Panagia,* I pray, *help him, and help us during this time of uncertainty.* Great Lent has begun, and this period of "bright sadness," as we describe it in the Orthodox Church, certainly reflects all the intense emotions I feel during this time.

"Do you think," my priest asks us when we tearfully tell him about the screening test and our fears, "that the devil hasn't noticed how hard you're working right now and how far you've come in your marriage?" I look at my husband. My priest is right. Our lives have been full of hard seasons, struggles, disappointments, and other griefs, but we've been focusing on forgiveness, trusting God, and loving, even when it's hard. It's not always easy, but we know from our experience that the number one thing Satan seeks to destroy is the family. We can use this time to trust test results and fall into despair about our own family, or we can trust God and ask for His help as we learn to discern His will.

At night, I lie in bed and press the *milagros* cross the shopkeeper gave me again to my belly. In the far bottom corner of the cross is a tiny image of a little boy, one I hardly noticed before. Now the image jumps out to me like a beacon. I rub my thumb over its shape, close my eyes, and say a prayer for my own little boy's development. I think about the shopkeeper, too, and say a prayer for her. She might not even remember giving me this cross in a moment of selfless kindness so many months ago, but her generosity, spirit, and encouragement haven't left me, and I know with all my being that the kind of love she showed to me that day made a difference in my life.

I want my little boy someday to touch this cross with his tiny fingers and see all the places where I prayed for him. I want to tell him about the shopkeeper and her shop of Marys, tucked away in the New Mexico mountains. I want to teach him to look for opportunities to love and bless others, just as she did with me. Miracles happen, I know. Healings happen. *Look at this year,* I tell myself. *They already have.*

"These things I have spoken to you, that in Me you may have peace. In the world you will have tribulation; but be of good cheer, I have overcome the world" (John 16:33).

I drift to sleep with the cross still against my belly, tucked between the warmth of our dog Lucy and my husband. Outside in the night, the buds on the pear trees break through the darkness and explode into white.

❋ TWELVE ❋

Creation

> *And I dream that these garden-closes*
> *With their shade and their sun-flecked sod*
> *And their lilies and bowers of roses,*
> *Were laid by the hand of God.*
> —DOROTHY FRANCES GURNEY[75]

AND JUST LIKE THAT: the entire world sheds its winter skin and rushes into spring.

Within a week's time, the white pear blossoms that exploded overnight give way to tender green leaves. As the leaves push forth, the blossom petals fall like snow in the lazy breeze, painting my neighbors' yards with the frenetic strokes of an Impressionist's brush. Spring rains follow, softening the ground enough that the tulips I'd forgotten I'd planted in the fall begin their spiral push through the soil. In the bright afternoon sun, they blaze like neon signs: electric orange, red-tipped yellow, a magenta that seems unreal. I watch them open their faces to the sunrise and arch their bodies toward the sun throughout the day before closing again at night.

The temperature warms enough that I can take my morning walks again. Twice one weekend, I pass by a tree near the playa in which a robin perches on exactly the same branch, singing his heart out with the morning sun. His call is clear and earnest, the most beautiful, hope-filled song. I stop to listen to him, amazed his tiny body can emit such a ferocious sound. In fact, the robins are suddenly everywhere. They dot the fields like little red-armored sentinels, marching ahead of me as I walk. "Where did you come from?" I ask one as I slow my pace. He tilts his head toward my voice, studying me with kohl-lined eyes before side-hopping out of my path and flying to a tree.

Back home, another robin sits by a half-cracked pecan on our front sidewalk, content to eat at his leisure in the sun. Another warms herself in the bare patches of earth in our backyard between sprints for insects. The abundance of these contented little creatures reminds me of Jesus' admonition to trust God for the basic things in life: "Look at the birds of the air, for they neither sow nor reap nor gather into barns," He tells His disciples in the Sermon on the Mount, "yet your heavenly Father feeds them. Are you not of more value than they?" (Matt. 6:26).

Like the birds of the air, I am reinvigorated by the West Texas spring. I long to be outside, shoving my hands into dirt and feeling the good strain of gardening work in my muscles. Our backyard is a small square of earth, but I try to cultivate it with beauty as much as my body and budget will allow. One weekend I rake the leaves out of the rose beds while my husband mows the first unruly shoots of grass. The work exhumes long-hidden smells of earth: musty, rich compost, the sharp smell of cut green grass. When we finish those tasks, I press soaked morning glory seeds into forgotten corners of the yard and help my husband plant a new peach tree in one of the coveted sunny spots.

"You'll be lucky if you get one peach on this tree," the home improvement store clerk told us as she checked us out, but we don't mind her pessimism. The little pink blossoms on the spindly tree are promising, and if this year has taught me anything, it's that there's always hope.

In the past, I viewed this precious little square of backyard as a sanctuary for my family, a secret garden of sorts, hidden from the street by the high fence and overgrown Texas lilac that came with the house. This year, however, I want it to be more. I want to dedicate my garden to Mary.

Several years ago, when we first moved in, only box hedges filled the garden spaces. With the help of a truck and chain, we ripped those out, and I planted rose bushes indiscriminately: different ones depending on the color of the blossom and the sale price. I wanted something wild and messy and full of color, like a child's finger painting. I've learned since then what kind of home roses really need, and it only seems appropriate that Mary should find a place here, too, since she is so often featured with flowers in iconography. I ask for her blessing as I scrape and fertilize the earth around the roses and clip off last year's exhausted branches.

As I carefully lean down to pull weeds, I also think about what else I'd love for this garden to become: a place of wonder for the little one growing in my belly. I want to teach him about the mason bees and how they've made their homes in porch holes with the rose leaves they've cut. I want to rake his tiny hands across the overgrown rosemary and honeysuckle by the old shed and hold them to his nose. *Breathe in,* I want to say. *How does it smell?* I want to point to the quick blue dragonflies and monarchs on the late-summer gladioli and show him how to watch for the single hummingbird that lingers in the canopy of crepe myrtle. I want to lift him to touch the wind chimes and move their paddles back and forth so he can hear them sing. I want to teach him how to listen for the early-morning chirp of the cardinals crushing sunflower seeds in the bird feeder—so different from the sharp demands of the blue jays as they dive for June bugs.

And even if we get one peach on our tiny tree, I want him to taste and see that the Lord is so very good.

My deep hope for all these things fills me with such longing I can hardly bear it. I stop and press a hand against my belly, grown larger even in one week, to be sure this is still real.

"You okay?" my husband asks me across the grass. I nod. White blossoms drift down around us like snow. I can't feel the baby moving regularly yet, but something twinges inside me. I remember his dancing on the ultrasound a few weeks ago.

"More than okay," I say.

Somewhere above us, a mourning dove coos for a mate, and a few early honeybees dart among the rosemary blossoms.

In heaven and on earth, all of creation rejoices.

※

THE FIRST POEM I LEARNED as a child wasn't a nursery rhyme or a song. It was actually a stanza from Dorothy Frances Gurney's 1913 poem "God's Garden," cross-stitched in blue and pink on a piece of framed cotton that hung in all the houses of my childhood:

Creation

The kiss of the sun for pardon,
The song of the birds for mirth,—
One is nearer God's heart in a garden
Than anywhere else on earth.

I know a garden isn't required to be close to God's heart, but I understand what Gurney was getting at. The first garden was a true expression of God's heart, creativity, and love for His human creation. He could have placed Adam and Eve anywhere, I suppose, but He chose to shelter and provide for them in the most beautiful plot of earth possible: Eden.

I love to read the scant details about Eden and how "out of the ground the Lord God made every tree grow that is pleasant to the sight and good for food" (Gen. 2:9 NKJV). I try to imagine acres of swaying, flowering, sweet-smelling fruit trees, buzzing with honeybees and birds. How beautiful that all must have been, and how beautiful Adam and Eve must have been, partaking of the air, food, water, and light so perfectly created for them, until sin separated them from this communion of body and spirit with their Creator. The colors, tastes, and variety of beauty that must have existed in Eden are unimaginable. In fact, everything in and outside of Eden that God made was good, as God Himself is good (Gen. 1:10).

I am reminded that an echo of the first humans' experience still lingers today. When I smell a rose blossom, or add the rosemary to a dish, or let the sun sink into my skin, it all becomes a part of me in some way. Even the tiniest drop of honeysuckle nectar I pull from a blossom and place on my tongue mixes with pollen and dust and is incorporated into my cells. I read the baby now tastes what I eat when he swallows tiny amounts of amniotic fluid, tinged with flavors of my last meal. It makes participating in the Eucharist each Sunday so much more important. When I take the Body and Blood of Christ into my body for "healing and sanctification," as we read in the pre-communion prayers, the Eucharist is not only incorporated into my body but becomes part of my unborn son's body, as well. We participate together.

I may not live in Eden, but I certainly have a version of it, even in this small place.

WHEN MY HUSBAND AND I finish our yard work, I sit back and survey my labor and decide that it, too, is good—at least a good start. I don't make any of this grow; the mystery of that belongs to God Himself, but I at least try to honor and care for it. I watch as Lucy, newly freed from the confines of the house, runs to each corner of the yard, inspecting with her sharp nose what we've disturbed from beneath the irises and leaf piles. As my husband runs the sprinkler and the smell of water and earth wafts around us, a warm satisfaction floods my blood. It is fitting to devote this space to Mary, to whom we owe a part of this creation, too.

Frederica Mathewes-Green has a wonderful insight about Mary and her role in our creation: "Everything earthly about Christ's body," she writes, "everything that's *us*—was supplied by and through Mary's own body."[76] It's a profound thought, and one I think most people miss. God provides divinity, but without Mary's physicality, the mundane reality of her flesh, bones, and biology, we would be without the Incarnation of Christ. In other words, Christ *needed* a human mother to be born; without Mary, Christ wouldn't have the full humanity

He possesses and ultimately shares with us. The first few lines of the Nicene Creed, spoken at every Divine Liturgy, affirm this belief: "I believe in one God, the Father Almighty, Creator of heaven and earth, and in one Lord Jesus Christ . . . through whom all things were made."

Everything we are in atom and energy, Christ is also, and through Christ's death, *all of that* is redeemed, including the physical world. Unlike gnostics and a few other sects, Orthodox Christians do not believe that the body or the physical world is "bad" or something that must be destroyed or escaped for our salvation. It is all good, just as God is good, for He made it. A great deal of blood and ink has been spilled over the millennia to defend this theology, for as the author of 2 Peter tells us, as hopeful Christians we "look for new heavens and a new earth in which righteousness dwells" (2 Pet. 3:13). This is not a *different* creation, however; it is *this* creation, the one God created and through Christ's great sacrifice will restore to the original state for which it was intended.

This is perhaps why the old cross-stitched poem resonates so much with me. I long to return to that place, as God longs to return us to Himself. It's hard work to create any kind of lush garden in the Southwest, but I try anyway. The earth, grass, and unruly patches of weeds I fight every year in the blistering heat are one way that I connect with Him in that sense. Maybe the dust that settles over us when the March winds blow mercilessly is just a far-flung echo of that Eden, but I sense God's original intent in that, too. It's just one other way that I can approach Him.

In fact, we can't help but approach Him through the physicality of our world. It's our human experience. We can't divorce ourselves from it, no matter how much we may try, because God created us to be physical creatures and to commune with Him in matter as much as in spirit. The Garden of Eden was very much a physical place, with heat and coolness, dust and water, shadow and light, and a myriad of growing things. We were made from its very foundations—"for dust you are, and to dust you shall return," God reminds us (Gen. 3:19 NKJV).

Likewise, the very elements of the Eucharist—bread, water, wine—are a reassurance that Christ's saving Presence in the world is one of matter. We don't consume the mere *idea* of Him; we take in the whole physicality of what He is. In fact, we honor and recognize the sacredness of the physical, so much so that early Christians risked their lives to "gather the bloody remains of martyrs, even when it endangered them to do so."[77] The body is sacred and deserving of honor because it is God's creation and the vehicle through which He showed Himself to the world.

And without Mary becoming the Mother of Christ, we might not have seen this at all.

※

A FEW WEEKS PASS, AND I unexpectedly spend more time in my backyard than I intended. A pandemic has gripped the world, and everyone at my university is told to work from home for the rest of the semester. I set up a desk on my porch and try to adjust to a new routine and the challenges of doing a face-to-face job entirely online as I look out onto the greening grass. As my husband and I read about the worst cases of illness around the world, the pandemic slowly creeps into our community and claims its first victim. We pray, check in with friends and family, and stay home as required, but it's especially difficult because we can't go to church as usual. Almost all services have been relegated to the internet with strict limitations on when we can participate in the Eucharist. For now, we can partake, but we don't know how much longer that will last.

Feeling especially vulnerable in pregnancy, I find myself praying to Mary even more. I'm not worried for myself as much as for my husband, whose work brings him in contact with all corners of our community, for my family and friends, and for my unborn child. I take my mother groceries and stay home as much as possible. All over message boards on social media, people share news of the ill, concerns for jobs greatly affected by efforts to slow the pandemic, and fears for the future. As the Divine Liturgy for the Annunciation arrives and I watch my priest deliver the service on social media, I am struck by how the celebration is nearly *lost* in what's happening. It's so easy to focus on the bad news that the good news is almost buried.

And what good news it is.

The Feast of the Annunciation is a small break in the usual fasting rigor of Great Lent to celebrate the Virgin's conception of Jesus and the message brought to her by Gabriel. In a time when everything feels out of control and so much of my day-to-day activity rests in the decisions of civil and ecclesiastical authorities, Mary's words echo back to me yet again: "Let it be to me according to Your word" (Luke 1:38). I can do nothing except trust in God and know that He's at work, even in this.

I pull out my copy of the Akathist Hymn and read through some of the lines I haven't read since almost a year ago, when this whole journey started. They take on an even richer meaning. I can't be in church on Friday nights to celebrate this service anymore; it, too, is being streamed online. But the praise Romanos gives to the Virgin feels new and fresh:

> *The Creator revealed a new creation when He presented Himself to us, who were made by Him; blossomed from a seedless womb, He kept her as she was, pure, so that we, seeing the Miracle, may praise her saying:*
> *Hail! O Flower of incorruption . . .*
> *Hail! O Tree of delectable fruit, nurturing the faithful . . .*
> *Hail! To you, who give birth to the Redeemer . . .*[78]

The entire Akathist Hymn to the Theotokos "focuses on a particular area of Christian theology that had been thoroughly tested in prior centuries, the full humanity and divinity of Jesus Christ," Mathewes-Green writes. "Here the goal is not so much understanding God in a rational way as directly experiencing him. This worship," she continues, "starts with the assumption that God is present throughout Creation, sustaining our every heartbeat, hearing our every thought, perceptible in the beauty and love we encounter in the material world."[79] Even in this world, with dust and weeds and viruses, He is here, and He is good. And we give thanks to Mary for her role in the birth of His Son, which makes our lived—and redeemed—lives possible.

It's a wonderful, intricate balance of honor and praises. As I sit on my porch and read the rest of the Akathist Hymn, the chimes sing, and the last of the pear blossoms blow across the patio. I close my book and set it to my belly, and I wait in the gray-green color of the garden for my husband and Lucy to join me.

❉ THIRTEEN ❉

Guides of Grace

But to each one of us grace was given according to the measure of Christ's gift.
—EPHESIANS 4:7

They fly in a silent, dark spiral just above my house. Red-tailed hawks, dozens of them grouped in a kettle, the tips of their outstretched wings burning copper in the late afternoon sun.

My neck hurts from craning so long watching them. As soon as two or three cycle out of view over my neighbors' trees, another two or three appear from the southwest over the roofline. I spin on my patio and follow their flight as they glide through the air in an unhurried wave. The kettle rides the thermals, those updrafts of warm, quick air that keep the hawks in flight so easily they barely have to move their wings. Unlike the Canada geese, my boisterous winter friends, these regal raptors fly in utter silence, without even a scream to draw the eyes upward. It was only the flash of their passing shadow that made my husband and me look to the heavens and gasp.

I have never seen anything like this in all the years I've lived in West Texas. Spotting one or two hawks along a rusty fence line near the canyons or in the sky above the mesquite-heavy roll of plains is not uncommon. But dozens of them flying into view over the busy and distracted miles of city blocks is a bit of magic. The gift of it humbles me as it transforms our little patch of ordinary afternoon into a moment of awe. God's admonition to Job pops into my mind: "Does the hawk fly by your wisdom, and spread its wings toward the south?" (Job 39:26 NKJV). No, it doesn't. Grace as wide as their wingspans infuses the moment.

A thermal shifts, and the rest of the hawks plummet out of my view. My pulse quickens as I see something else follow them: a Mississippi kite, her golden, bespotted body lit from beneath by the afternoon sun, following the hawks to catch a free ride on the thermals, too. She is one bird so visually different from the rest, soaring on the joy of the sky right along with them.

Another vision of grace.

※

I WAIT ANXIOUSLY IN THE lobby at my next doctor appointment. In the few weeks that have passed since my last awful appointment, I've come to a resolution about the news my doctor gave us on that terrible afternoon. I can't let the *what-if* of our test results color the rest of my pregnancy. I want my baby to feel my joy and not my fear, and I don't want to be consumed by worry these last months. I want to enjoy this time that may only come once.

Still, I'm not quite ready to interact with the talkative nurse who so horribly bumbled the delivery of the test results, so I tap my feet and steady my breath as I wait to be called back, hoping she isn't the one I have to see. She and I both need grace there. I breathe a sigh of relief when a different nurse escorts me back to my examination room.

My doctor walks in a few minutes later, and I am happy to see her. A middle-aged woman with a soft gray bob and kind, observant eyes, my doctor is relatively new to my town and—I learn later—will be taking over the entire birth center where I plan to deliver. I didn't know anything about her when I was hastily told to choose a doctor at my first prenatal appointment. "She's new," the office receptionist told me when I asked for a recommendation, "but she's very good. She's a maternal-fetal specialist." I didn't know what that was yet, but it sounded good to me.

Her first name is also Mary.

Today, I notice something else about her: a small, gold disc with a hammered cross hangs on a chain around her neck. A Christian symbol. I didn't notice it the last time I was here, when I was talking to her for the first time through the tears of bad news.

It's only been two weeks since I last saw her, but she sits down and starts speaking right away.

"I've been thinking about you a lot," she begins. "Really, the only reason I wanted you to come in today was to see how you are doing." Another moment of grace. I exhale a breath I didn't know I'd been holding. I realize I have been more nervous about this appointment than I let on, and I have an overwhelming urge to reach out and hold her hand because it means so much that she's been thinking of me.

"I've been thinking about you, too," I tell her, and I had been. Through the difficult weeks of fear and worry that the baby might have a disorder of some kind, the kindness my doctor offered me at my first appointment has clung to me. She'd answered all our questions in the best way she could and spoke patiently and optimistically to two parents who were scared. She'd even given me her cell phone number and told me to call or text her anytime with any questions I had. I hadn't felt the need to, but I hadn't forgotten the slip of paper with her information carefully printed in her handwriting, paperclipped in my work planner on my next appointment date. "I wanted to thank you for being so *kind* to me the last time I was here," I say. This makes both of us tear us up.

"I also wanted to apologize to you about how your last appointment went," she continues. This statement surprises me. "You know, we gave a name to something that maybe didn't need to be named at all." She explains that it's not always good how much medical technology and information we have access to and that everyone has genetic and biological "additions and subtractions" that make us who we are: little details that shape our personality, behavior, and development that we'd never know about ourselves unless we'd had some test run, as I had done. "But that's not the whole of who we are," she concludes.

She tells me a story of her first early years as a resident on a Native American reservation in the Dakotas. "I was the only doctor," she said, "and I was serving this entire community with a pharmacist and a single nurse." This nurse, my doctor explains, knew all the tribes and families within their area. "At the end of my residency, she gave me a gift: a beautiful piece of beadwork art for my stethoscope." The craftsmanship and detail were exquisite, my doctor tells me, and the work almost perfect, except for one tiny detail.

"In the midst of this white beaded background was a single orange bead. It was so out of place." My doctor thought it might be the nurse's artistic signature or something like that. "So I asked her about it. Why was this one bead here in an otherwise perfect background?" I lean in, enraptured by my doctor's story. She has had me come today at this specific appointment time, I know, so that she can talk with me longer than usual. She's not in a hurry and keeps her hands resting in her lap as she talks.

My doctor chuckles.

The bead, it turns out, was a purposeful aberration.

Her nurse, Mary says, got stern with her and said, "Only *God* is perfect.'" My doctor looks at me then, and I understand. Her nurse had placed that orange bead there, the outlier in the midst of an otherwise perfect background, to remind my doctor of who the real Creator is. "There is no perfection in human beings or in our genetic makeup," she continues.

She glances at my neck, where a small charm of the Theotokos hangs on an equally simple chain. It was my Valentine's Day gift from my husband. "I don't know what your faith background is, but I'm Catholic, and at mass on Sunday the sermon was about loving people and just being happy. And you know, that's really all that matters here. This little guy is going to have a great life and a great childhood because you love him."

She's absolutely right. I love him more than I can express already, and thinking about our life together as a family makes me cry big, sloppy tears. Mary dabs at her own eyes and laughs that she was always told not to get emotional with her patients, but how could she not when she's working with mothers and babies and life? She tells me other stories of hope and lessons she's learned in her career, of patients and people who've all illustrated that "life is big and messy and great." She guides me to a profound sense of peace and gratitude, and I cling to the moment, knowing that Mary the Mother of God is as present in this room today as she was nearly a year ago in that New Mexico shop, and in every interaction I've had since I began my search to meet her in my daily life.

We end the appointment with me on the examination table again, smiling and talking as Mary's ultrasound wand glides over my belly.

A little hand comes into view on the screen. My doctor pauses the video so I can take a photo with my phone to show my husband.

My son's tiny hand raised to the screen, as if to say hello. One palm, no bigger yet than my own fingerprint, with five little fingers, fearfully and wonderfully made.

※

IN PSALM 5, THE PSALMIST writes:

> *Give ear to my words, O Lord, consider my meditation.*
> *Give heed to the voice of my cry,*
> *My King and my God, for to You I will pray.*
> *My voice You shall hear in the morning, O Lord;*
> *In the morning I will direct it to You,*
> *And I will look up."* (Ps. 5:1–3)

This psalm is read as a morning prayer, one of the fixed psalms of the First Hour prayers in the Orthodox Church. It is a request for guidance through the day, and historically, it is the prayer the priest in ancient Israel would use to prepare the offering of the sacrifice. The Psalmist makes a confident promise to God: *To You I will pray. You will hear my voice in the morning, and I will look up.* The "looking up" is a sign of faith, for the Psalmist expects his help to come from God.

I keep looking up, too. Back home after my appointment, I look up to the sky, where the steam of a passing jet has left a long arc of white horizon to horizon, a halo framing the heavens. By now the red-tailed hawks will be circling in the bright afternoon heat of the canyons, far beyond the city. Some might alight at the highest point they can before pushing off into the thermals again, guiding the rest of nature skyward.

I remember a long hike I took a year ago by myself through the Sierra Blanca Mountains of New Mexico. The morning was cool, and I wanted the kind of long walk that made my legs ache with the joy of being alive. At a bend in the trees, I looked at my map, a simple colored brochure I'd found in a local shop. I could either veer left and head down to a small lake, making a simple two-mile loop back to my car, or I could head right toward the tree line for a seven-mile hike that would take me further into the backwoods. I decided on the longer route. What I *didn't* want, however, was to miss the crucial guidepost farther along in the hike, marking the split in the path that would either keep me on the seven-mile loop or lead me into a ten-mile trek through the mountains and back down to the water.

In the dazzling, sapphire-blue morning, I looked for lizards and listened to the birds as I hiked along the path, keeping time by what I knew to be my normal hiking pace.

The mountain air was so sweet and clean that I filled my lungs with it in great inhalations. I wanted to bottle that fragrance and take it home with me. I paused beneath ponderosa pines to take in the views, but always I kept my eye out for the crucial bend that would veer me back to the water. My pacing was good, and the hike not overly strenuous. *I'll be done in time for lunch*, I thought as I hiked. But the guidepost with its painted path numbers marking the way never materialized.

An hour passed, and I felt myself moving further into the mountains, far beyond the lake and my car below. Under the shade of a limber pine, I compared the brochure map to the map that materialized intermittently on my cell phone, now out of range of consistent service. Somehow I had gotten on the ten-mile loop, and I was now at a point in the hike where turning back would take just as long as going forward.

I remember thinking, *This isn't the path I planned to take.* How many of these unplanned paths there have been in life! So many times I thought I had things "right" in my life and was on a road headed to a clear destination, but I found myself on a different path entirely. Sometimes this was due to my own choices, and other times circumstances were out of my control. Missed markers, unexpected detours, and roadblocks to my plans have been frustrating and downright disappointing, but when I look back, I see that they resulted in surprising discoveries, moments of beauty, and humbling lessons that advanced me toward a deeper spiritual discipline and love in my life. "For My thoughts are not your thoughts, / Nor are your ways My ways," the Lord reminds me in Isaiah 55:8 (NKJV).

Perhaps this was one of those moments. By now, the sun

was overhead and lunch a passed dream. What else was there to do now but go on?

I kept my feet on the path, no wider than my own boots and carved into the mountain by rain and whoever—or whatever—else had walked this way. Bears roamed these woods, though, and I was alone. I kept my eyes sharply attuned to my surroundings, startling at every cracking twig and windy creak in the trees overhead, and berated myself for my grand idea. How did I miss the guide marker? Was it even there to begin with? What silly woman finds herself on a ten-mile hike alone?

Prayers, of course, were with me, but so was something else: the overwhelming feeling that perhaps I was lost. The path I thought was my way forward looked eerily similar to other paths crisscrossing the dry mountainside. With no guide markers, at times I didn't know if I was really on the right path at all.

How many times I have *also* felt this in my life, especially in instances like this when I thought I could just go it alone. Trudging through a portion of the Sierra Blancas—tired, hot, and anxiously looking for any confirmation I was headed in the right direction—only illustrated how easily I take my eyes off the True Path, almost always when I don't intend to. It's only in a moment of crisis, when I am faced with who I am, how much I've strayed, and how needy I am, that I realize my weakness and utter dependence on God. This changes the terrain of my prayer, too, from one of rote repetition into a prayer of presence. I am present in my need and my fear, and God is present in that, too. "The fact that we are present in a situation alters it profoundly because God is then present with us through our faith," Met. Anthony writes. "Wherever we are . . . we can recollect ourselves and say, 'Lord, I believe in you, come and be among us'."[80]

I hiked on, remembering that even in my lostness when I believed I was without a guide leading the way, God was with me. *Lord, I believe in You. Come and be with me.*

At the top of a ridge, the trail broke onto a flat plateau scattered with fallen trees, cinquefoil, and small yellow wildflowers blooming in sun. Tall trees—the kind that survive at the very tops of mountains in the thinning air—swayed with the wind and filled the air with a gentle hum. It must have blocked out all other sounds, for as I wound my way through a dense section of undergrowth, I startled a doe. We were so close I could see the gleam of moisture on her black nose and eyes. In one fluid motion, she swung her head in my direction and leapt out of my way, across the trail and north, disappearing into the shadows. I hardly had a moment to collect myself before two others, hidden somewhere behind her in the trees, followed. Their escape was like an exhalation of breath. Whose, I'm not sure. I stood stunned for a moment and then smiled to myself.

Soon, the trail turned south in their direction and sloped downward again, back toward the glittering lake I'd left so early that morning and my waiting car.

*

THIS AFTERNOON, I SIT IN the quiet of my backyard and my Mary garden now blooming with roses, Russian sage, and the growing fruit of our little peach tree, and I breathe into the movements of my child.

The baby kicks now, and it is the most wonderful feeling in the world. A soft *thump–thump* accompanies my days and sends little waves across my belly when I'm still. I put my hand to where I imagine his little feet must be and feel the tremors. He has his own routines, and I'm not alone anymore at night when I can't sleep, for he seems to sense I'm awake and starts kicking. The pattering and swishing of his little body serve as a guide that he's still there, still developing, and that our story is still being written. I wonder how Mary must have felt when the Christ Child started kicking in her womb. I am sure her joy was the same.

I think about all the guides I have been shown in this past year, both subtle and great: the mercy of my conversation with Mary, my doctor; the hawks flying overhead, showing me the invisible thermals swirling all around me; the movement of emotion in front of the Theotokos icon; my baby dancing in black and white, and now in real time against my hand. All of these things are quiet whispers, coming together to guide me to something more holy, if only I would pay attention to them.

This time searching for Mary has been no different. All my questions about her—my quest to know and understand her better as an Orthodox convert—have themselves been an arrow pointing the way toward a deeper, richer, more challenging spiritual development. This time has not been without pain, but as Martin Laird writes in his beautiful book *A Sunlit Absence: Silence, Awareness, and Contemplation*, "As growth takes place, pain occurs. This is true of life generally and abundantly so of the life of prayer. Prayer deepens by way of ordeal."[81] All love deepens by way of ordeal, I would add.

So many guideposts have appeared over this past year, guiding me toward Mary and a greater understanding of God. I think about the pear blossoms falling, the geese, my trinity of foxes from last spring, the shopkeeper in New Mexico, my long walks around the playa, and the story of Diveyevo Convent. I sigh as I remember my struggles with my mom, our grandpa dying, and in the midst of that grief the news our baby was coming. The hawks above, the falling leaves, the shadows of the pronghorn deer: all of it is imbued with an overarching sense of grace. I know without a doubt the Mother of God is a part of all of it, praying for me and the whole world in a voice I can't hear, and that she still points the way toward a deeper understanding of faith, which grounds me in what God has done for me and continues to do for the entirety of humanity. All of it undeserved but given anyway.

"Is there a richer and stranger idea in the world than grace?" writer Brian Doyle asks in his essay "Grace Notes."[82] "Only love, grace's cousin, grace's summer pelt," he answers himself.

It is love that has led me here, I know. And love that will lead me on, no matter what happens.

I lean back and stare up into the blue and watch for the next sweep of wings.

❋ FOURTEEN ❋

Mourners

*Sing praise instead of mourning, so that in place of
mourning you may receive a blessing.*
—SAINT JOHN OF THESSALONICA[83]

THEY GATHERED AROUND HER, a ragtag bunch of motley travelers. Some wore the tunics they'd had since Christ's admonition to "take nothing for the journey" (Luke 9:3); others wore the adopted fabrics of the faraway places where they had been preaching. But these apostles hadn't traveled weeks through hostile lands and rough storms to get to Mary's bedside. They'd been taken up all at once, tradition holds, "each . . . in a cloud"[84] and transported miraculously at the same moment to the low-lying walls of her modest home, shaded now with the heavy darkness and vigil that accompanies imminent death.

John the beloved, to whose care Mary had been entrusted by Christ Himself as He died on the Cross, arrived first. Then followed Peter, Paul, and the rest of the apostles, except ever-endearing and logical Thomas, according to another tradition. He arrived last.[85] When all the apostles had gathered, however, they embraced and cried aloud, touching each other's weathered faces and graying hair, missed dearly after so much time. Astonished at the miracle that had brought them all together, they prayed "that it may be known to us why God has brought us together."[86] But John, knowing the reason already, shared it with his brothers: Mary, the Mother of Jesus, was soon to depart this Earth.

When the time came, they gathered around her bed and leaned in, each one of these men who had encountered God Incarnate and witnessed miracle upon miracle, glory upon glory. They gazed on the humanity that had brought Him forth. Here was the woman who had made it all possible so many years before with her simple *yes*. Emotion flowed like the living water they'd been drinking and spreading across vast swaths of the world: grief at her passing and joy at the hope of the resurrection. As she departed in the fading light of day, she echoed the humble words she'd spoken so many years before when Gabriel revealed she was to bear the Redeemer of the entire world: "Who am I, lowly one, that I have been counted worthy of such glory?"[87]

In her humanity, she bore God human life, which subsequently led to the human death He willingly accepted on the Cross, a final death that trampled down death forever more.

Now it was time for her own. But "Death, long seen as revolting and hateful, is now praised and called blessed," for miracle after miracle would flow from her for ages to come.[88]

That Mary lived *and* died, we cannot forget.

※

I HAVE BEEN DREAMING ABOUT my father. It makes perfect sense that I should, pregnant with a little boy who still in his mystery might carry some of my father's traits. But still, the dreaming surprises me.

My father will have been gone almost exactly ten years by the time this little one arrives, and enough time has passed that I have learned to live without seeing him every week, hearing his stories, and laughing at his jokes. I suppose I thought I could handle even this new season without my dad, but having a child thrusts me forward and then back again in emotional whiplash. I want the people I've loved who are gone to meet my son, and so I am hurled back through the years to the time when they were alive, kindling fresh grief that they aren't physically here with me now.

One dream in particular lingers longer than usual this morning. I am meeting my mom and dad at a bus stop. They have arrived together after some journey. The bus lurches to a stop along a street bright with color that I don't recognize, and my mother disembarks first. She says something I can't remember and walks away. Frustration flares. I have been angry at my mother in my dreams lately, which unsettles me. In waking hours, I do what I can to manage our relationship and to work on acceptance, forgiveness, and release. But in my dreams, we are disconnected.

I want to talk to her in my dream, to get her to understand me, but then my father emerges. I am shocked, for in my dream he steps off the bus with a confidence and smile I hadn't seen him wear for years when he was alive. He looks healthy, happy, and as if he knows exactly why he's here. "Go easy on your mom," he tells me in the dream, and I know this is him speaking to me through my own psyche, but perhaps also from somewhere beyond. And this realization makes my dream sharpen and crack; I know now this is a dream and that he isn't really standing there in front of me whole. Knowing it isn't real, I hug him anyway, and beneath my hands I can still feel the shape of his neck and back and the rough knit of the faded polos he always wore. I know that the moment is fleeting and the timeline of my dream doesn't line up with what my slowly waking brain knows is real.

So I pull him tighter and whisper into his ear, "Yes, but I know some things you don't know." What I mean is: *I know what is going to happen to you. I know how hard life is going to be for us when you leave. I know that you will die.*

"I know that he will die," he says about himself, echoing my thoughts. I pull back but see in his face he isn't surprised at all by his own statement. What rational sinews have held this dream together begin to stretch and break, and my father dissolves.

I slowly drift back into the familiar darkness of my bedroom. Tiny, bubble-like kicks of my child, waking in the womb with me, pull me the rest of the way across the wide abyss of sleep and into the present. I touch my belly and breathe into the space where he is kicking. This is real, I know.

I am glad for the dream: glad to see my dad once more and for the rare chance to feel the solidness of his presence beneath my hands, a sensation so missed all these years he's been gone. But I am also grieved, for it surfaces things I hadn't really let myself think about yet in the busy day-to-day of work, chores, and life: What a good grandpa my dad would have been. How much I wish he was here now. How he will never meet my child this side of Paradise. How much I know my son and he would have loved each other, and, perhaps, how much my dad already does.

Remembering my dad's tender, kind personality and how he interacted with his great-nephews when they were young, I can only guess at the amount of love my son and he would have shared. Part of my job as a parent will be to cultivate that love, to teach my son about his grandpa so that when they meet, God willing many years after I have left this earth, they will already recognize each other.

I know this is true: a reality exists somewhere beyond the boundaries of earthly time that has no beginning, middle, or end. A reality that is and always has been, one I will encounter someday. It is the state of being in the full glory of God and everything He is. But in the darkness this morning, I feel a little like Thomas, somehow having arrived late and needing to see the proof of this joy: the nail holes in my Savior's hands and feet, the empty tomb, all my brothers gathered together again. I wish fervently then, in a way I haven't in a very long time, that my dad was still alive.

I let the full weight of ten years of missing him descend like a cloud and silently mourn, the *pat-pat* of my baby's kicks against my womb tethering me to the moment.

❈

IT WILL BE AUGUST SOON, and two things hang on the horizon like approaching summer rains: the birth of my son, and the Fast and Feast of the Dormition of the Mother of God.

The Fast of the Dormition is a two-week season in the Orthodox Church in which we prepare for Mary's death, burial, and miraculous reception into heaven by her Son. The purpose of the fast is to give us time to eliminate earthly distractions—our appetites (both physical and mental), empty leisures, and accompanying traits that separate us from God—and focus on her role in our salvation, and prepare for her departure. When we cut out certain kinds of foods and behaviors, it creates space for something else to fill, and the goal is to fill this space with edifying things: spiritual focus, true knowledge of ourselves, and a return to God. Although this is a shorter fast than Great Lent, it's no less difficult, for it reveals, as Fr. David Smith writes, "my slavery to my appetites, my spiritual immaturity, my total reliance on the grace of God. . . . The essence of fasting," he succinctly surmises, is "that I might encounter myself."[89]

The fast culminates in the Feast of the Dormition each year on August 15 (August 28 on the Julian calendar), the day we celebrate her reception into heaven. This is a season long celebrated in the Orthodox Church, having been established in the sixth century. In the excellent book *On the Dormition of Mary: Early Patristic Homilies*, Brian Daley writes in his introduction that "the story of Mary's dormition . . . began to be told perhaps as early as the late fourth century" and that "by the second half of the sixth century . . . [it] had come to be accepted as part of Christian tradition."[90]

"Dormition," or *dormitio* in Latin, means "falling asleep" and is the term used consistently in Orthodox teaching when describing Mary's death or end. In fact, "falling asleep" is the phrase Orthodox Christians use when describing all deaths, for it references the temporary state in which our bodies—and not our souls—remain until the resurrection. As St. Andrew of Crete wrote in his second homily on Mary's Dormition:

> It is death's tyranny, real death, when we who die are not to be allowed to return to life again. But if we die and then live again after death—indeed,

> live a better life—then clearly that is not so much a death as a sleep ("dormition"), a passage into a second life, which brings us as migrants from here to there and sends us on our way by giving us complete release from earthly cares.[91]

True death does not encompass us entirely, for our souls never die. Rather, we wait for the "glorious liberty" that is the hope of the resurrection (Rom. 8:21) and the reunion of our bodies and souls in the presence of God, as we were always meant to be.

The Dormition of Mary is important for several reasons. First, her death is the example of what all Christians hope for. As a human being, "the death that is natural to the human race even reached as far as Mary."[92] Mary died a natural death, like any human being, and her soul was received into heaven by Christ not *just* because of who she was (simply His Mother) but also because of the virtuous life she lived and the role she plays now as "intercessory and patron for the rest of humanity."[93] The goal of every Christian should be to live such a life of virtue that when our death arrives, we may not fear it but rejoice. Even in her death, as in her whole life, she subjugated herself to God's will.

However, her Dormition takes on an even more important meaning and spiritual significance when we look at it in the context of the hope of the resurrection that Christ promises to all people. Some tradition teaches that after Mary's burial, her body disappeared after three days, "for she had been taken away by Christ, the God who became flesh from her, to the place of her eternal, living inheritance."[94] Like St. John of Thessalonica, other early, major homilies by the Church Fathers on Mary's death, burial, and transition into the presence of God almost always describe the event in "hallowed euphemisms": her "change of state," "change of dwelling," and even "transferral" into God's glory.[95] They avoid the language of *resurrection*, which is reserved for Christ, but hint at a greater hope about "Christ's Paschal Mystery itself" and what He promised all believers:

> *Because her humanity stands closest to the humanity of Jesus, which has passed through death to a new, indestructible life suffused with his own divinity, because she is still "one body . . ." with Jesus, Mary is the first to experience the full transformation of body and spirit—the "divinization" of what is human—that is promised to everyone who becomes "one body" with him in faith and baptism.*[96]

This traditional teaching about her death points back, as all focus on Mary should, to Christ. The fast and feast serve as times to contemplate, through her human example, what it means to live a Christian life, what it means to die in the context of those beliefs, and what we should hope for as human beings ourselves: the promise of what Christ has already offered the world through His sacrificial death and Resurrection.

It reminds me, too, of the "woman from the crowd" who called out to Jesus as He preached on spiritual power and spiritual warfare in Luke's Gospel. "Blessed is the womb that bore You," she cried out in her exuberance over what He was saying, "and the breasts which nursed You!" But Christ returned, "More than that, blessed are those who hear the word of God and keep it!" (Luke 11:27–28). He wasn't discrediting or putting down His Mother here; rather, He was stating a principle that God doesn't just bless people because of who they are related to. Anyone who "hear[s] the word of God and keeps it" is blessed.[97] His Mother served as the greatest example of that, the most "blessed among women" (Luke 1:28).

This is the tradition that is alive and celebrated in the Orthodox Church. We remember that everyone mentioned in the Bible had a beginning, a life, a purpose, and an ending. The lives of the saints were kept alive through oral tradition, the records of the early believers, and the teachings of the early Church. Mary's story is no different. Brian Daley summarizes this wonderfully when he writes that all the major early church homilies on Mary's Dormition were "not so much a particular aspect of Biblical teaching or Church dogma" but instead "a statement of the Church's impassioned hope for humanity itself, as called in Christ to share, beyond death, the glorious fullness of the life of God."[98]

This is what the Fast and the Feast of the Dormition of the Theotokos direct us back to: hope. We remember we will die. We prepare for the wrenching grief of separation. We pray for those who have gone before. But ultimately, we hope in the resurrection and life to come, knowing that death's real tyranny can't hold power over us forever.

We sleep but for a little while.

※

EARLY ONE MORNING, I RISE to walk and pray, and I see the moon gleaming through my bathroom window. I haven't seen it in weeks and am excited to have it light my way this morning. However, when I step outside, it is shrouded by long bands of linen-white clouds.

The air is still cool this morning, and the wind that has

quickly blown in the clouds above me feels like silk against my skin. As I pass beneath the neighborhood shin oaks and maples, the wind roars in the trees, heralding a change.

Earlier this week, my cousin sent me a message that he wanted to give me an old guitar of my dad's. My family is full of musicians, and my father was a music teacher for years. This was the guitar he played when he was very young. "I've always felt that it should stay in your family," my cousin tells me, and this touches me. I don't have a lot left from my dad, but I do have his love of music, so my cousin's generosity gives me great joy. Although the guitar is in bad shape and not playable, it will be something special I can share with my son, handed down especially to him.

"We have a lot to share with this little guy about his grandpa in heaven," I tell my cousin. And we do. There will be stories, and there will be music, I decide. Lots and lots of music. And we will all nestle in the bed together and listen to music until we fall asleep.

We'll hold onto each other through whatever dreams we dream until we wake again in a place where there is no pain, nor sorrow, nor sighing.

Only Life everlasting.

❊ FIFTEEN ❊

The Return of the Prodigal

*But when he was still a great way off,
his father saw him and had compassion,
and ran and fell on his neck and kissed him.*
—LUKE 15:20

A YEAR LATER, AND MY car is pointed west along that needle-straight road again. The midmorning sun peeks from the last of the clouds, remnants dissolving from a summer rain the night before. It is interesting that this sky is almost identical to the sky I saw twelve months ago when I traveled this road alone into New Mexico. The same aching blue stretches above, but it's not the same. This a different day. A different year.

A different me.

This time, I am not alone with the radio, my thoughts, and the small icon of the Theotokos in my cup holder. My husband sits beside me today, his calm and quiet presence giving me comfort. I am so happy he's with me. I'm driving again, but this time, it's because the driver's seat better accommodates my growing belly and the accompanying body aches that come from the life growing inside me, not because I am the only one headed west on this bright morning.

We are returning to the small village in New Mexico where I spent a few days last year reading, writing, and asking how I could meet Mary in my life. It's not a trip that is a gift to me after a difficult year; this trip is a "babymoon," the last time my husband and I will spend together as a family of two without work distractions before the baby comes. It's also a return to the place where I feel this journey of mine began, and there is so much I want to share with my family that brought me joy before: hikes through the Sierra Blanca Mountains, Italian cream sodas at the coffee shop along the river where I wrote, the tiny cabin where I rested and prayed. And, of course, I want to go back to the stucco building with bright green trim where I met the shopkeeper and found myself face to face with mercy.

I want this more than anything else, in fact: to introduce the shopkeeper to my husband, show her my belly, and tell her how much her kindness a year ago influenced my life. I want my husband to see her beautiful work, her mother's handmade jewelry, and all the lovely Madonnas lining the room. I have brought with me the cross with the hammered *milagros* that she gave me, and I want to pull it out of my purse and tell her which tin charms I touched as I prayed and how Mary was there to help me through it all.

Most of all, I want to tell her that miracles are real and that she was right: none of this past year could have happened any other way.

I think about all this as I drive, sing, and chatter to my husband. New Mexico is just starting to reopen after the first wave of the pandemic, including the shops along this village's main street. This is the only weekend we could come given work schedules and safe travel guidelines for my pregnancy. Internet research doesn't reveal much about my friend's store, and I hope sincerely she is there.

Soon the sun burns away the overcast sky and reveals a searing blue. It is hotter this weekend than it was a year ago, but the mountains will still offer some reprieve from the heat. As the Texas highway I drive narrows into the slow, two-lane road that will take us into New Mexico and up into the mountains, the landscape changes from golden buffalo grass and blue grama to sun-bleached patches of sand, desert saltgrass, and creosote bush. In these plains outstretched like an open palm, the earth is almost the same color as the sun. We see pronghorn deer again, their arcing horns and dotted faces elegantly contrasted against their white hinds. No fawns hide beneath their mothers' shadows today, however. Instead, the babies all belong to the darker animals. Longhorn calves skip and play alongside their mothers, their hides black and shiny as tar. Above us, nestled in the crooks of telephone poles, we see huge mesquite-twig nests of Chihuahuan ravens, the inky heads of chicks peeking out while mothers scan for raptors.

My own baby kicks and bounces in response to the drive and our voices, and I am amazed, as always, by the working of his little body inside mine. All of this feels like a priceless inheritance, and I am like a prodigal returning home, determined and humbled, asking to be in my Father's presence once more.

Not wanting to squander a thing.

JESUS' PARABLE OF THE PRODIGAL Son is the third parable in Luke's Gospel. He tells it to His disciples to drive home the message that "there will be more joy in heaven over one sinner who repents than over ninety-nine just persons who need no repentance" (Luke 15:7). Luke begins this series with the parable of the lost sheep. "What man of you," Jesus asks His disciples, wouldn't leave his flock "in the wilderness" to go after one sheep that went astray, and when it is found, call "together his friends and neighbors" to rejoice? (15:4, 6). The sheep is valuable, He implies. So valuable, in fact, that a man who recognizes its importance would leave the security of his flock to enter a rugged and harsh land to find the lost sheep. He would take a chance, in other words, because that one sheep had gone astray and deserved to be returned to the safety and care of the group. It is loved and valued that much.

Likewise, Jesus continues this theme with the parable of the lost coin. He likens the experience of finding one lost sheep to the fervency with which a woman would "sweep the [whole] house, and search carefully" until she found a valuable silver coin she'd lost (15:8). Again, the coin is so valuable that when it is found, "she calls her friends and neighbors together" to rejoice (15:9).

And finally, to really make His point (in case His disciples still aren't getting it), Jesus tells the parable of the Prodigal Son. This parable appears only in Luke's Gospel and is a beautiful story rich with emotion. A younger son decides he wants to leave his family home and live a different life, so he asks his father for his portion of his inheritance. To split an inheritance would have been disastrous in these times, for it would have diminished the land and income not just of the father, but of the entire family, who depended on those resources to survive. However, the father grants his younger son his portion, a reference to the free will that God always allows His creation.

The younger son, prideful and foolish, squanders his inheritance quickly in a faraway land, and when a famine arises, he comes into a time of great need. Utterly destitute, he takes a job feeding pigs, a deplorable task to the Jews, for pigs were despised as unclean animals. The younger son suffers such great hunger during this time that he would eat the food given to the pigs— an act of complete despair and degradation—if only anyone would offer it to him.

Finally coming into his right mind, the younger son realizes that in his father's house, even the "hired servants have bread enough," and he could return home to work as one—if only his father would accept him back (15:17).

And oh, how he does. The passage that always brings tears to my eyes is 15:20: "And [the younger son] arose and came to his father. But when he was still a great way off, his father saw him and had compassion, and ran and fell on his neck and kissed him." The father saw the son *first*. In fact, he never stopped looking toward the horizon. He scanned it every day for his son's figure, hoping that something would finally call his son home, and when an emaciated, ragged, and humiliated version of his boy appeared, the father felt such joy and compassion flood into him that he ran to his beloved child with open arms. The father ran so far, in fact, that he met his son in that same wilderness into which he had disappeared, and the father fell onto him when he reached him, kissing and hugging him in an uninhibited display of affection, and dragged him back home.

This is what God does. He doesn't just expect us to find Him; He comes to us through love, direct action, and the efficacy of others that we might be found and return to His presence. He looks for us every day. He enters into the wilderness of our lives to search for us. He carefully combs through the world to find each one of us who has been forgotten or neglected. And when He finds us, He places us on His shoulders in an outpouring of emotional love and brings us home, clothing us in good things and calling to the angels, saints, and all of heaven to rejoice, for He has found that which was lost.

I think again about the heartrending lines of the Prayer to the Virgin Mary from the Akathist Hymn I prayed in front of her icon during Great Lent: "But, as the Mother of the Merciful God, mercifully show compassion unto me, the sinner and prodigal." I am the prodigal, too. How many times do I squander God's gifts, my heavenly inheritance, and turn away from my true home to pursue my own will and desires, not caring how my actions affect others or the world? The Orthodox believe we are saved in *community*—not individually—and that every action, sin, and decision we make creates a ripple effect that has an impact on others and, indeed, the whole of creation.

This prayer reminds me of that lowly state in which I so continually find myself and asks for Mary's compassion and help to "open for me the merciful depths of His loving kindness . . . and guide me to repentance." She wants nothing more than for every human being to return to Love's true embrace, and the prayer reminds me to start the journey home and look for God, too, who is ever scanning the horizon for my figure, waiting for my return.

The Return of the Prodigal

A QUICK DRIVE AROUND THE village reveals only a few open stores, so we spend the first few days resting and relaxing in our cabin as much as possible. However, on our last day in the village, we get up early to walk the sleepy main street. This is the coolest morning in the mountains so far, and a light breeze whispers through the surrounding pines, merging with the sound of the murmuring river below. I want to go by the shopkeeper's store once more to see if she has opened up. It is a weekday, and tourists have begun to arrive in town. We walk slowly, giving me time to navigate the inclines and crosswalks, and finally, we arrive at her brown-and-green storefront. I walk toward the welcoming door where small pots sit with spring flowers, a sign someone has been here, but am met by disappointment.

The store is locked, and almost everything inside is gone. Brown paper covers the glass cases where glittering jewelry once sparkled among the lights. The walls are stripped bare of their crosses, and the Madonnas no longer watch customers come and go from their places of honor. Only a few *regalos*, little gifts, and one large, colorful wooden icon of Mary lean against the windows to indicate a business is even here. It is closed up "indefinitely" with no notice of when it will open again.

I place my hands on the windows and peer into the shadows of the store, overwhelmed with discouragement. I knew there was a chance she wouldn't be here, but still, I had hoped. I wanted so badly to see the shopkeeper again, but I cannot. At least not today. It is only this Mary waiting for me in the window, her face and eyes painted with soft, calming hues, who meets me. I don't realize it in that moment as we turn to walk away, but it is fitting that she's there. She is, after all, the reason for this journey.

Perhaps it's impossible to really return to the same places we've left. The memories I have of this little village, my interactions, and the experiences I had here hang unchanged in my mind's eye like the crosses the shopkeeper hung floor to ceiling. But in reality, places and people change. This village and, in fact, the entire world are not the same places they were a year ago. Likewise, I am not the same person I was when I walked into her store. I was a different person by the time I walked out, so profound and healing was that human interaction.

When the prodigal son returned home, he was different, too. His father remained the same, as God always does, for it is we who change and not God. Humans are the inconsistent ones, ever influenced by our emotions, ego, and desires. But the prodigal son's home was not the same place he left, either, for he came back a changed person: full of repentance, humility, and a painful awareness of what he'd squandered and nearly lost. He saw his old home with new, grateful eyes. It was not the place he'd taken for granted so many years before. He'd been blind to that. *This* home—the one he returned to—he wanted so desperately he was willing to relinquish the title of *son* and become one of his Father's hired servants.

I walk away from the closed shop and accept the mystery that today I'm not meant to see the shopkeeper. I will find some other way to thank her. I resolve instead to write her a letter and tell her about this book and how all her kindness accompanied me on this long and wonderful year searching for Mary. Perhaps I'll see the shopkeeper again someday. Perhaps on that special day, a baby boy will be in my arms instead of my belly, or walking with me, his hand in mine, down the street. I pray the world is healed by then.

I turn around as we leave and catch one last glimpse of the Mary in the window, her tall frame keeping a peaceful and silent watch over the sleepy village. I pray, too, she'll still be here when it all reawakens.

※

WE LEAVE THE VILLAGE TO go on one last hike. A few miles north, we find a small, unhurried lake and a trail that takes us along mountain slopes, hushed pines, and the lazy tripping of a cold stream. The breeze from the morning has brought in clouds that make the two-and-a-half mile walk easier. I can't do as much physically as I used to, and the growing person in my belly keeps us at a stroll instead of a hike. "Our bodies humble us," Fr. David Smith notes. "Who can imagine that God took one for Himself? And yet He did, a gift from His Mother to Him and to us. . . . She understood that the essence of the Incarnation was humility, and she took this virtue for herself in order to teach it to the infant, the toddler, the boy, and the young man, our Lord Jesus Christ."[99]

I am greatly humbled by my body these days, and I think of Mary and the terrain she traversed as she carried the Christ Child. In the heat, dust, and desiccating wind of a West Texas summer, I can imagine only a small portion of what her experience must have been like. I hobble along at a slow pace and think of the gift of her humility and how she took on this virtue for the benefit not only of Christ, but of the entire world. At every turn in her life as Christ's Mother, she embodied this, denying her own will and ego to teach the Son of God and guide Him to be who He ultimately became as man. "Where else would He have learned it?" Fr. David plainly asks.

And how I have learned it, too, all these long and beautiful and painful and magnificent months. I realize it, then, beneath the passing shadow of a towering fir as I walk: it's been the *humility* of this experience that's driven every prayer, question, tear, sigh, and ultimate praise toward God and my own learning and spiritual growth. By opening myself up to this experience, admitting that I knew virtually *nothing* of the Theotokos as a convert and asking for her help to guide me toward a better understanding of her and her role in my faith, I have found myself in a place rich in spiritual inheritance. Like the needle-straight road leading me here, my prayer, study, and praise of the Theotokos have given me a fuller participation in the Church, the Body of Christ, and a deeper love for God.

Where else would I have learned it?

The trail dips down into a narrow valley. We pass by blocky gray boulders covered in yellow lichen guarding the entrance to where the creek tumbles into waterfall. Ground squirrels with tails patterned like zippers scurry in the underbrush and jump across stones. Overhead, a solitary raven caws as it passes to higher places, and hummingbirds buzz and chirp like electric fairies. The air is light and sweet here, the creek a soothing lullaby. I stop along its banks to dip my hands into the cold water and pat the back of my neck to cool off. As we head back toward the lake, swallows with emerald backs fly over the cattails and skim the surface of the lake, catching insects.

As we climb out of the valley and wind our way back to where we started, I thank God again for this time. I thank Mary, too, for the role she's had in this and everything she has taught me so far. "The Theotokos is not God," Fr. David reminds me, for "she cannot be in all places at all times. But she can become for us a *fount of incorruption* . . . a *tower of safety* . . . and a *portal of repentance* when we continually cry out to her and gain her attention by our prayers and devotion."[100]

I hope through my prayers and devotion, I have gained her attention, as Fr. David writes. I believe I have, and I have faith that she's heard me, as this year has shown me. I will keep asking and praying for her intercession and help, no matter what comes next in life.

At the last bend around the lake, we see a tree full of red-winged blackbirds, the same kind I see at home flitting around our playas. They call to each other boldly, grabbing our attention, and glide from the tree into the reeds below. We can't help but notice them, so sure and loud are their cries. I watch them come and go for only a moment, for the afternoon stretches like a sleepy child in the shadow of the mountain.

We walk the rest of the gravel path to our waiting car.

It is time to go home.

Epilogue

I*N THE DARKENED ROOM*, an unexpected quiet fills the air. The only sounds are the low murmurs of the hospital staff as they move about the room. Outside, the September sky is pitch black, pierced only by the waning moon. We thought my baby would be born in August when the moon shone fully in the sky, but this sweet baby has taken his time, deciding to arrive (with a little help) at last on this night.

It feels appropriate that he comes now, for so many dark mornings I spent walking and praying to Mary. My pocket icon of her sits on the bedside table, and her gaze overlooks the delivery room, which is as dim as the moon outside. The low lighting brings a sense of calm to an otherwise electric moment. My son has begun his descent into the world. Everyone's eyes are fixed to the glowing monitor in the corner, its yellow and blue bars separating my vitals from my son's. My heartbeat blinks strong and steady on the screen, but my baby's fluctuates dramatically.

A contraction begins, and his heart rate falls. The tension in the room increases.

"It is normal," I am told. "We are monitoring how well he tolerates each contraction."

But in the silence, I recognize how helpless I am. The

uncontrollable power of giving birth has overtaken my body, and I have no option but to surrender to it. My labor has been fast and intense, and a small fear skitters down my spine as I realize I can't control what's happening or how my baby responds to the shifting environment in which he now finds himself. I strain my eyes over my shoulder toward the monitor behind me, trying to make sense of the jumble of lines and numbers I see through the fatigue of my labor, but a warm, firm voice cascades over me.

"You don't worry about that. That's our job. You just focus on you." The Irish lilt of my doula's words comforts me, and I am reminded that I must trust, yet again. My hand spontaneously finds the pendants in the tangle of chains around my neck: the Virgin Mary and a guardian angel, both given to me by my husband. I am aware of my husband somewhere on my right, whispering that I am doing well, I can do this, but I am so tired it's hard for me to focus. I perceive someone else enter the room and hear my doctor tell her to make preparations.

It is almost time. Time, which has lost all meaning to me. The blinds in the room have been drawn, and I can tell from the glow of the parking lot lights that it is night, but I don't know the hour or how long exactly I have been in labor. Labor has transformed seconds into hours, pulling time so thinly it almost feels as if it is standing still.

The Protoevangelium of James tells that on the night Christ was born, Joseph, who went to find a midwife for the laboring Mary, observed time somehow standing still. In this beautiful passage, he is privy to the profound moment when Christ's birth alters the world around him:

Then I, Joseph, was walking, but somehow I did not walk. I looked up to the vault of the heavens, and saw it standing still . . . and the birds of the air motionless . . . And I saw sheep being driven, yet the sheep stood still . . . And I looked upon the water-brook and I saw the kids put their mouths down upon the water and not drink. And suddenly all things moved forward in their course.[101]

God's birth into a world governed by time transforms time itself as the laws of nature bend and break to the Creator who made them. It becomes clear to me that my perception of time is also altered as my son and I near our meeting. Soon we will cross the threshold of birth and enter a life with each other for which I have long prayed and waited. I know others have prayed and anticipated him, too, both here on Earth and beyond. Their faces skip across my mind: our families, anxious for news; my dear friends in my writing group who shared this journey; our intimate circle of friends; and the people at our church. I can't wait for him to meet them all, but in this moment, nothing else matters except his entry into the world.

A contraction ends, and another one begins.

It is time.

Mary's gaze from the bedside table remains ever steady, as outside, the moon seems to suspend its trek across the western sky.

※

FROM MY PORCH SWING, WE watch the leaves fall like confetti to the ground. The ornamental pears next door, which once exploded in blossoms of white, now swirl red in the wind. The maples across the alley glow a golden-rust, and all the other trees in our neighborhood turn from cool greens to warm oranges once more.

I point out each tree I can see to my baby as we swing and nurse, the November sky a halting blue against all this shifting color. He moves his gaze between my face and the play of shadow and light beneath the porch, and I wonder what he perceives as we swing and rock. Everything that has cycled before for me is new to him, and it makes me look at this glorious fall afternoon with fresh eyes.

I marvel at how so much is the same, yet also how so much has changed in such a year. In the constant unmooring of such change, God has ever remained faithful. "God is good all the time, and all the time, God is good," a friend once wisely told me.

And it is true.

However, in an unexpected drought this summer, the playas dried up. Without water, the geese have flown elsewhere, taking their wild calls with them. They don't fly over our house this autumn, heralding the new morning. I look into my baby's eyes, their blue-gray color reflecting my memory of those waters. I know that when the rains return, the playas will fill again, and perhaps by then he'll be old enough to walk with me down to the water's edge. There we will see the ducks and watch the morning light dance across the water, and I'll tell him about the Theotokos, the foxes, and all that came before him. Including Suzi.

Suzi, my dear friend, who died.

When she went into hospice after several months of unexpected illness, I called her, sure I wouldn't get through at such a crucial time. I expected the phone to ring, turn over to voice mail. After sending her a series of "I love you" texts,

I planned to leave a long voice message, hoping one of her daughters would play it for her. But Suzi answered, her voice sounding near and far away all at once.

"Brandi?" she asked.

"Suz . . . Suzi. Yes, it's me."

"Oh, I'm so glad you called. I was in the middle of texting you, but it was too long." I heard the weariness in her words, but her tone still conveyed the strong and proud woman she was. "It's time," she explained without me having to ask. "I'm ready. I have been thinking about you," she continued. "Everything you wrote." I thought about the pages of this book that Suzi read and the gentle advice and encouragement she gave over the years. I remembered how supportive Suzi was of my search for Mary, the Mother of God, and all the beauty she brought to my writing with her feedback. I wanted so badly for Suzi to get a final copy, to see my acknowledgment to her.

But I realized Suzi will soon see so much more.

"I've also been thinking about the baby," she continued with more effort, her words drawn out more slowly. This is what made my heart break. "Thank you for sending me his picture."

In my arms, my baby fussed. The news she was dying came in an email from one of Suzi's friends, and I had been feeding my son when I read it and called. She won't get to meet him. I won't get to call her again.

"Oh, Suzi." I choked. "What am I going to do without you?"

At the end of the line, in some room I didn't know, Suzi sighed. "I know. Do what you need to do over this. Scream, cry, jump off your roof if you need to." But I was already crying. My son squirmed and twisted more and pushed his tiny hands against my breast. I shifted him in my lap. "But when you're done with all that," she said, her voice suddenly turning firm, "get back to being a better person."

"I love you so much, Suzi. So much. And I'm going to see you again." It was futile, but I wanted time to stand still, to keep her on the line so that the moment wouldn't end. I didn't want to have to hang up and know that was the last conversation I would have with her.

"Oh, I know that. I love you, too. And those crazy ladies. Tell them I love them. And keep writing."

"I will," I said, thinking of our heartbroken writing group friends. "I promise, I will."

Finally, my son let out a frustrated wail.

"Oh," Suzi said, her voice full of wonder. "I hear him."

"I hear him, Brandi," she repeated.

✼

I WALK DOWN BY THE dry lake bed anyway, my son in a carrier against my belly. He looks up at the waving branches of the poplars and the elms and listens as I tell him about the Theotokos, and the foxes, and the wild geese, and Suzi. He listens to everything I say until he falls asleep against my chest and begins snoring—a soft, tiny sound one would almost miss if she wasn't listening.

Additional Reading

Wʜɪʟᴇ ʀᴇsᴇᴀʀᴄʜɪɴɢ ᴛʜᴇ Mᴏᴛʜᴇʀ of God, I found a wide variety of resources that added to the richness of my study. While most of what I recommend below are Eastern Orthodox references and definitely worth adding to any library devoted to the Theotokos, this list also includes other spiritual writing (including from different faith backgrounds), nonfiction, poetry, and even secular texts that shaped my understanding of the Virgin Mary and her place in the world today.

Books about the Virgin Mary

Archim. Maximos Constas (trans.), *Mother of the Light: Prayers to the Theotokos* (Columbia, MO: Newrome Press, 2018).

Holy Apostles Convent, *The Life of the Virgin Mary, the Theotokos* (Buena Vista, CO: Holy Apostles Convent and Dormition Skete, 1989).

Francis Johnston, *The Wonder of Guadalupe: The Origin and Cult of the Miraculous Image of the Blessed Virgin in Mexico* (Rockford, IL: Tan Books and Publishers, 1981).

Frederica Mathewes-Green, *Mary as the Early Christians Knew Her* (Brewster, MA: Paraclete Press, 2013).

Met. Isaiah of Denver, *Behold Your Mother: A Reflection on the Virgin Mary* (Denver, CO: The Greek Orthodox Metropolis of Denver, 2019).

Brian E. Daley (trans.), *On the Dormition of Mary: Early Patristic Homilies* (Crestwood, NY: St. Vladimir's Seminary Press, 1998).

Fr. George Papadeas (trans.), *The Akathist Hymn Preceded by the Brief Compline* (Daytona Beach, FL: Patmos Press, 2010).

Fr. George Papadeas, *Why Did She Cry: The Story of the Weeping Madonna* (Daytona Beach, FL: Patmos Press, 2000).

Fr. David R. Smith, *Mary, Worthy of All Praise: Reflections on the Virgin Mary* (Chesterton, IN: Ancient Faith Publishing, 2004).

Jacob of Serug, *On the Mother of God*, trans. Mary Hansbury (Crestwood, NY: St. Vladimir's Seminary Press, 1998).

Charlene Spretnak, *Missing Mary: The Queen of Heaven and Her Re-emergence in the Modern Church* (New York: Palgrave Macmillan, 2004).

Resources on Prayer

The Ancient Faith Prayer Book, ed. Vassilios Papavassiliou (Chesterton, IN: Ancient Faith Publishing, 2014).

Anthony Bloom, *Beginning to Pray* (Mahwah, NJ: Paulist Press, 1970).

Met. Anthony Bloom and Georges LeFebvre, *Courage to Pray*, trans. Dinah Livingstone (Crestwood, NY: St. Vladimir's Seminary Press, 1984).

Martin Laird, *An Ocean of Light: Contemplation, Transformation, and Liberation* (New York: Oxford University Press, 2019).

Martin Laird, *A Sunlit Absence: Silence, Awareness, and Contemplation* (New York: Oxford University Press, 2011).

Frederica Mathewes-Green, *The Jesus Prayer: The Ancient Desert Prayer that Tunes the Heart to God* (Brewster, MA: Paraclete Press, 2009).

Books about Orthodox Theology, Tradition, and Practice

These books include helpful sections on our understanding or reverence of the Theotokos.

Harry Boosalis, *Person to Person: The Orthodox Understanding of Human Nature* (South Canaan, PA: St. Tikhon's Monastery Press, 2018).

John T. Chirban (ed.), *Personhood: Orthodox Christianity and the Connection Between Body, Mind, and Soul* (Westport, CT: Bergin & Garvey, 1996).

Saint Herman of Alaska Brotherhood, *Our Thoughts Determine Our Lives: The Life and Teachings of Elder Thaddeus of Vitovnica*, trans. Ana Smiljanic (Platina, CA: St. Herman of Alaska Brotherhood, 2017).

Stanley S. Harakas, *The Orthodox Church: 455 Questions and Answers* (Minneapolis, MN: Light & Life Publishing, 1987).

Fr. George L. Papadeas (trans.), *Greek Orthodox Holy Week & Easter Services: A New English Translation* (Daytona Beach, FL: Patmos Press, 2016).

Met. Anthony of Sourozh, *God and Man* (London: Darton, Longman and Todd, 2004).

Benjamin D. Williams and Harold B. Anstall, *Orthodox Worship: A Living Continuity with the Synagogue, the Temple, and the Early Church* (Chesterton, IN: Ancient Faith Publishing, 2018).

Other Works

While these aren't necessarily Orthodox resources or references on the Virgin Mary, I found them to be thought-provoking and inspiring to my own writing. I've included a brief description of why you may enjoy them.

Russell M. Hart, *The Icon Through Western Eyes* (Springfield, IL: Templegate Publishers, 1991). This book introduces Westerners to icons and is written especially for a Protestant perspective.

Rainier Maria Rilke, *The Life of the Virgin Mary*, trans. C. F. MacIntyre (Westport, CT: Greenwood Press, 1947). This is a

Additional Reading

beautiful series of poems about the life of the Virgin Mary.

Philip Zaleski (ed.), *The Best Spiritual Writing Series 1998–2013* (New York: HarperCollins Publishers). This series includes some of the best spiritual poetry, essays, and stories published each year in one volume.

Exploratory Questions

Chapter One: Tears

1. The author describes in detail the setting in which she became Orthodox. Why does place have such an impact on how we experience our faith? How might you experience your faith differently if you lived in a different part of the country or world?

2. How do the icons in the author's church affect her when she looks at them? What visual representations of your faith do you keep around you? How do they help you?

3. The author admits that even after ten years of being Orthodox, there is still so much she doesn't understand and wants to learn. What questions do you still have about your faith? How could you begin to find those answers? Who could help you with your search?

4. The author's journey to "meet" Mary almost immediately begins with an emotional experience, an acknowledgment of her neediness, and the effect of direct prayer. Have you ever had a humbling experience like this? If so, what happened? What did it teach you?

Chapter Two: Strangers

1. The author discusses how she begins to pray more consistently to God, the saints, and Mary. How does prayer to those who've gone before benefit us? How is this similar to or different from asking friends and family to pray for us?

2. What request does the author make of Mary on her trip? How is that request fulfilled or answered? When have you petitioned God, the saints, or others for help in your life?

3. What do you think motivated the shopkeeper to minister and talk so openly to the author? Have you ever had an experience of divine intervention like this? If so, what happened? How did it affect or change you?

Chapter Three: Prayers

1. What unconventional prayer rule does the author establish? Do you have a prayer rule or routine that you follow? Why do you think prayer is so important in the author's journey to learn more about Mary or in any journey we begin in order to get closer to God?

2. What does the story of the Diveyevo Convent teach the author? Have you ever been on pilgrimage or visited a holy site? If you could go anywhere, where would you go and why?

3. Why was the early Christian prayer to Mary so important? What could be the benefit of praying some established prayers, such as the Jesus Prayer, the Prayer to the Virgin Mary, and others already written down and used for millennia? Are there any other special prayers that you pray?

4. What are some immediate challenges the author encounters in her new prayer routine? What are some things we should consider when we pray and attempt to enter the presence of God?

Chapter Four: Vessels

1. In this chapter, the author describes the conflict she experiences between who she is and who she wants to be in her daily life. What are the most challenging aspects of your work, career, or daily life? What would you change about yourself or your circumstances to deal with those challenges better?

2. How important was Mary's free will in her decision to say yes to God? What might have happened if she had said no to God at any point in her life? Are there times when you've ignored God's will in your life or wanted to force your will onto Him? How did that go?

3. What do we learn about Mary's character and the type of person she must have been through her interaction with the archangel Gabriel? What virtues does she begin to exhibit that make her a model for all Christians?

4. When have you cooperated with God's will? What happened? What was the outcome?

Chapter Five: Mothers

1. The author writes about her struggles with her mother and how those struggles are reflected in her relationship with Mary. Do you identify with some people from the Bible, saints, or even the Persons of the Holy Trinity (God the Father, Jesus Christ the Son, and the Holy Spirit) more closely than others? Why?

2. In what ways have you asked those people for help in your life?

3. Why is the title *Theotokos* so important in Orthodox Christianity? What does it say about Mary's role in our salvation and her relationship to Christ, His Incarnation, and His purpose in the world?

4. Do you have a difficult relationship with someone in your life? If so, how do you manage it? What is one thing you can do today to change that relationship for the better? If there is nothing you can do to change it, what else can you do for that person or yourself?

Chapter Six: Holding Lightly

1. In this chapter, the author discusses a difficult decision she makes in her family. Have you ever been in a similar situation with someone you loved? If so, how did you handle it? What did that experience teach you about yourself and that relationship?

2. Why is Mary rarely, if ever, featured alone in Orthodox icons? What does this teach us about Orthodox theology and Mary's relationship to her Son?

3. When the author tries to "hold lightly" to her own fears and worries, what happens? What are some areas of your life you can "let go" or hold more lightly, allowing God to have more control? What holds you back from doing this?

Chapter Seven: Dryness

1. In this chapter, the author discusses a difficult period of dryness she experiences in her spiritual life. Have you ever gone through a period like this? If so, what was it like? How did you get out of

it? If you still feel that way, what are some things you can do to move past it or seek help?

2. How does the author ask for help in her personal struggles? How does Mary help her? What does the author learn she was missing all along in this experience?

3. How often do you incorporate gratitude into your life? How might you better give thanks for all things in your daily living?

Chapter Eight: Friends

1. Why are the author's friends so important in her journey to discover Mary? How have your friendships assisted you in some of the most important times of your life, and in particular, your faith?

2. What does a close reading of Luke's Gospel reveal to us about the inner workings of Mary's heart and mind? What details did you learn about her in this chapter you might not have known before?

Chapter Nine: Miracles

1. In this chapter, the author describes a series of miracles she either reads about or experiences in her own way. How are those miracles defined? Have you ever witnessed something miraculous—or even extraordinary—in your life that defied explanation? Have you ever experienced a healing of the soul that was equally miraculous?

2. Christ's first miracle at the wedding at Cana is a pivotal moment in Christianity. What role did Mary play in Christ's revelation to the world? Why was their interaction at this humble wedding so important? What does this teach us about being believers?

Chapter Ten: Wives

1. How are the concepts of *betrothal* and *engagement* different? Why was betrothal taken so seriously in the ancient world? What were some benefits and challenges of living in a culture in which betrothal had such important implications?

2. Why were Mary's virginity and vow of chastity so important? What does this chapter teach you about Mary's betrothal to Joseph you didn't know before? How does this change your view of Mary and Joseph's relationship?

3. In what ways can you rely less on your own understanding and instead better follow the will of God in all your relationships?

Chapter Eleven: Sorrows

1. Why is Mary considered both the greatest of mourners and the greatest of intercessors in the Orthodox Church? What does Mary's profound suffering over her Son teach us?

2. Think of a time you have suffered greatly. How does suffering in life change or affect our faith and relationship with Christ and God the Father?

3. When you find yourself suffering over something, to whom or what do you usually flee? Is there a better or different way you can approach your suffering?

Chapter Twelve: Creation

1. Orthodox Christians believe that Christ is fully God *and* fully human. What did Mary provide for Christ's humanity? How does her role in this directly affect us today, both as believers

who partake in the life of the Church and as individuals living in a created world?

2. What can nature teach us about God's providence and presence in our lives? Are there any natural spaces, plants, or animals you enjoy? How could you incorporate more of the natural world into your daily life?

3. How do you see God present in the mundane details of the ordinary world?

Chapter Thirteen: Guides of Grace

1. How does the grace and mercy of the doctor affect the author? Have you ever experienced an unexpected moment of mercy or met any guides of grace in your life? If so, what happened and how did it affect you?

2. What does the author learn about perfection in this chapter? What does this chapter teach you about the idea of perfection?

3. Has there ever been a time in your life when you've been lost, either physically or metaphorically, or found yourself on a path you never expected? How did you handle that situation? How were you able to get back on track? What is something you can do when you find yourself in that lost place again?

4. When you look back over the past year, what signs or guideposts do you recognize have led you to the current moment?

Chapter Fourteen: Mourners

1. Why is the term *dormition* or *falling asleep* used instead of the word *death* in Orthodox tradition? How does this change your view

or understanding of what happens to us when we die? What is "death's tyranny, *real* death" to which the author refers?

2. What does the story of Mary's death teach us about our hope in Christ? What of her life and death can we emulate in our own lives?

3. What people have you lost in your life, and how can you keep their memory and spirit alive with those you love?

Chapter Fifteen: The Return of the Prodigal

1. Jesus often spoke in parables to illustrate spiritual truths. These stories, clothed in the details of daily living, taught His listeners important lessons, but they also served to challenge His audience to think more deeply and take personal responsibility for their understanding of what He was preaching. Which parables of the Bible are your favorites? Why?

2. The parable of the Prodigal Son is layered with themes of repentance, love, and forgiveness. What other themes do you find in this parable? How do the father's actions conflict or contrast with the Jewish ideology of the day or even with how you might have responded if these were your children? In your opinion, what makes this a powerful parable?

3. Have you ever tried to return to a place you loved or recreate an experience you once had? How did it go? What did that attempt teach you?

4. What was the greatest lesson or virtue the author learned in her search for Mary? What's been the biggest thing you've learned by way of reading this book?

Endnotes

1. Adapted from the Prayer to the Virgin Mary in Fr. George Papadeas (trans.), *The Akathist Hymn Preceded by the Brief Compline* (Daytona Beach, FL: Patmos Press, 2010), pp. 103–105.
2. Fr. David R. Smith, *Mary, Worthy of All Praise: Reflections on the Virgin Mary* (Chesterton, IN: Ancient Faith Publishing, 2004), p. 7.
3. A. M. Casiday, *Evagrius Ponticus* (New York: Routledge, 2006), p. 5.
4. Mary Karr, *The Art of Memoir* (New York: Harper Perennial, 2015), pp. xx–xxi.
5. Met. Anthony Bloom and Georges LeFebvre, *Courage to Pray*, trans. Dinah Livingstone (Crestwood, NY: St. Vladimir's Seminary Press, 1984), p. 17.
6. Smith, p. 7.
7. *Symeon the New Theologian: The Discourses*, trans. C. J. de Catanzaro (Mahwah, NJ: Paulist Press, 1980), p. 31.
8. For a complete version of this prayer, please see the opening pages.
9. John of Kronstadt, *My Life in Christ: Or, Moments of Spiritual Serenity and Contemplation, of Reverent Feeling, of Earnest Self-Amendment, and of Peace in God*, trans. E. E. Goulaeff (London: Castle and Company, 1897), p. 80.
10. John of Kronstadt, *My Life in Christ: The Spiritual Journals of St. John of Kronstadt*, ed. Nicholas Kotar (Jordanville, NY: Holy Trinity Publications, 2015), p. 12.
11. Anthony Bloom, *Beginning to Pray* (Mahwah, NJ: Paulist Press, 1970), pp. 31–32.
12. Frederica Mathewes-Green, *Mary as the Early Christians Knew Her* (Brewster, MA: Paraclete Press, 2013), p. 87.
13. Mathewes-Green, p. 86.

14 Mathewes-Green, p. 88.
15 Bloom, *Courage to Pray*, p. 18.
16 Bloom, *Courage to Pray*, pp. 16–17.
17 Papadeas, *Akathist Hymn*, p. 13.
18 Smith, p. 48.
19 Prayer of Met. Philaret of Moscow, in *The Ancient Faith Prayer Book*, ed. Vassilios Papavassiliou (Chesterton, IN: Ancient Faith Publishing, 2014), p. 10.
20 Mathewes-Green, p. 94.
21 Mathewes-Green, pp. 94–95.
22 Met. Isaiah of Denver, *Behold Your Mother: A Reflection on the Virgin Mary* (Denver, CO: Greek Orthodox Metropolis of Denver, 2019), pp. 14–15.
23 Ibid.
24 Ibid.
25 Smith, p. 30.
26 Ibid.
27 Smith, p. 52.
28 Stanley S. Harakas, *The Orthodox Church: 455 Questions and Answers* (Minneapolis, MN: Light & Life Publishing, 1987), p. 331.
29 Ibid.
30 Smith, p. 12.
31 Harry Boosalis, *Person to Person: The Orthodox Understanding of Human Nature* (South Canaan, PA: St. Tikhon's Monastery Press, 2018), p. 80.
32 Boosalis, p. 81.
33 Mathewes-Green, p. 118.
34 Smith, p. 52.
35 *Elder Joseph the Hesychast: Struggles—Experiences—Teachings*, trans. Elizabeth Theokritoff (Mount Athos, Greece: Monastery of Vatopaidi, 1999), p. 149.
36 Mathewes-Green, p. 118.
37 Ibid.
38 Bloom, *Beginning to Pray*, p. 33.

39 Archim. Maximos Constas (trans.), *Mother of the Light: Prayers to the Theotokos* (Columbia, MO: Newrome Press, 2018), p. xvi.
40 Bloom, *Beginning to Pray*, p. 26.
41 Ibid.
42 Constas, p. 5.
43 Constas, p. 7.
44 Constas, pp. 7–8.
45 Bloom, *Beginning to Pray*, p. 27.
46 Bloom, *Beginning to Pray*, p. 76.
47 Met. Anthony of Sourozh, *God and Man* (London: Darton, Longman and Todd, 2004), pp. 169–170.
48 Fr. George Papadeas, *Why Did She Cry: The Story of the Weeping Madonna* (Daytona Beach, FL: Patmos Press, 2000), p. 78.
49 Met. Anthony, *God and Man*, p. 167.
50 Smith, p. 14.
51 Met. Anthony, *God and Man*, p. 166.
52 Met. Anthony, p. 167.
53 *The Orthodox Study Bible* (Nashville: Thomas Nelson Publishers, 1993), p. 215.
54 Met. Anthony, *God and Man*, p. 168.
55 Met. Anthony, *God and Man*, p. 169.
56 Met. Anthony, *God and Man*, p. 170.
57 Ibid.
58 Papadeas, *Why Did She Cry*, p. 90.
59 Marcus Jastrow and Bernard Drachman, "Betrothal," http://www.jewishencyclopedia.com/articles/3229-betrothal (accessed May 23, 2020).
60 Holy Apostles Convent, *The Life of the Virgin Mary, the Theotokos* (Buena Vista, CO: Holy Apostles Convent and Dormition Skete, 1989), p. 25.
61 *Life of the Virgin Mary*, p. 53.
62 *Life of the Virgin Mary*, p. 55.
63 *Life of the Virgin Mary*, p. 58.

64 *Life of the Virgin Mary*, p. 59.
65 *Life of the Virgin Mary*, p. 60.
66 *Life of the Virgin Mary*, p. 64.
67 Ibid.
68 *Life of the Virgin Mary*, p. 70.
69 *Life of the Virgin Mary*, p. 67.
70 *Life of the Virgin Mary*, p. 69.
71 Ibid.
72 Scott Cairns, *The End of Suffering: Finding Purpose in Pain* (Brewster, MA: Paraclete Press, 2009), p. 110.
73 Cairns, p. 102.
74 *Life of the Virgin Mary*, p. 373.
75 Dorothy Frances Gurney, "God's Garden" (1913), in J. Franklin Willis, *Of Roses and Poets* (Walla Walla, WA: Xlibris Corporation, 2006), p. 11.
76 Mathewes-Green, p. 123.
77 Mathewes-Green, p. 15.
78 Papadeas, *Akathist Hymn*, pp. 36–37.
79 Mathewes-Green, p. 126.
80 Bloom, *Courage to Pray*, p. 56.
81 Martin Laird, *A Sunlit Absence: Silence, Awareness, and Contemplation* (New York: Oxford University Press, 2011), p. 6.
82 Brian Doyle, "Grace Notes," in Philip Zaleski (ed.), *The Best Spiritual Writing 2001* (New York: HarperCollins Publishers, 2001), p. 48.
83 John of Thessalonica, "The Dormition of Our Lady, the Mother of God and Every-Virgin Mary," in Brian E. Daley (trans.), *On the Dormition of Mary: Early Patristic Homilies* (Crestwood, NY: St. Vladimir's Seminary Press, 1998), p. 53.
84 John of Thessalonica, p. 55.
85 Andrew of Crete, "On the Dormition of Our Most Holy Lady, the Mother of God," in op. cit., p. 225.
86 John of Thessalonica, p. 55.
87 John of Thessalonica, p. 63.

Endnotes

88 John of Damascus, "On the Dormition of the Holy Mother of God," in op. cit., p. 196.
89 Smith, p. 99.
90 Daley, *On the Dormition of Mary*, pp. 9–12.
91 Andrew of Crete, pp. 118–119.
92 Andrew of Crete, p. 121.
93 Daley, p. 26.
94 John of Damascus, p. 67.
95 Daley, p. 27.
96 Daley, p. 32.
97 *The Orthodox Study Bible*, p. 169.
98 Daley, p. 35.
99 Smith, p. 114.
100 Smith, p. 78.
101 Mathewes-Green, p. 65.

BRANDI WILLIS SCHREIBER IS a published author of poetry, nonfiction, and award-winning fiction. A longtime native of West Texas, she writes between two horizons, where the visible expanse of the Texas plains and the invisible expanse of the human heart and faith meet. A convert to Orthodoxy, she holds an MA in English with an emphasis in creative writing and poetry and a BA in English language and literature, both from Texas Tech University. This is her first full-length book of creative nonfiction.

Ancient Faith Publishing hopes you have enjoyed and benefited from this book. The proceeds from the sales of our books only partially cover the costs of operating our nonprofit ministry—which includes both the work of **Ancient Faith Publishing** and the work of **Ancient Faith Radio**. Your financial support makes it possible to continue this ministry both in print and online. Donations are tax deductible and can be made at **www.ancientfaith.com**.

To view our other publications,
please visit our website: **store.ancientfaith.com**

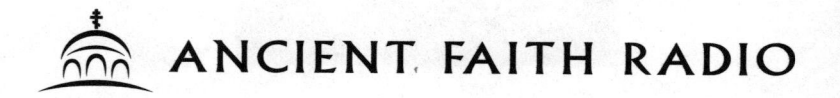

ANCIENT FAITH RADIO

Bringing you Orthodox Christian music, readings, prayers, teaching, and podcasts 24 hours a day since 2004 at
www.ancientfaith.com